LIFE INSURANCE: WILL IT PAY WHEN I DIE?

BY

THOMAS W. YOUNG

The contents of this work, including, but not limited to, the accuracy of events, people, and places depicted; opinions expressed; permission to use previously published materials included; and any advice given or actions advocated are solely the responsibility of the author, who assumes all liability for said work and indemnifies the publisher against any claims stemming from publication of the work.

All Rights Reserved
Copyright © 2020 by Thomas W. Young

No part of this book may be reproduced or transmitted, downloaded, distributed, reverse engineered, or stored in or introduced into any information storage and retrieval system, in any form or by any means, including photocopying and recording, whether electronic or mechanical, now known or hereinafter invented without permission in writing from the publisher.

Dorrance Publishing Co
585 Alpha Drive
Pittsburgh, PA 15238
Visit our website at dorrancebookstore.com

ISBN: 978-1-4809-9135-4
eISBN: 978-1-4809-9393-8

CONTENTS

DEDICATION v
PREFACE vii
INTRODUCTION xiii
AUTHOR'S NOTE xix
FINDING YOUR STYLE xxi

PART 1

Chapter 1: What is Life Insurance? 3
Chapter 2: Some history of the life insurance industry 5
Chapter 3: Universal Life Insurance and Index Universal Life 14
   Type A and B Policy. (See article in Appendix)
Chapter 4: Term Life Insurance 37
Chapter 5: Level Premium Term Life Insurance Policy 39
Chapter 6: Variable Life Insurance 44
Chapter 7: Whole Life Insurance 45
   How to Read the Annual Statement 52
   Table of Guaranteed Maximum Rates for Each $1000 of Term Insurance 64

PART II

Chapter 8: Opportunity Cost of Money 67
Chapter 9: Pension Maximization 73

Chapter 10: Reverse Mortgage 76
Chapter 11: Tax Savings 77
Chapter 12: Wealth Accumulation 81
Chapter 13: Disability Benefits 84
Exhibit #1 87
   Why Widows Are Left Destitute, The Loss of Their Spouses' Life Insurance Benefits, According to 25-Year Insurance Professional.
Exhibit #2 89
   Life Insurance Goal Planning Worksheet
Appendix A 91
   Terms and Definitions
Appendix B 112
   Important Provisions to Know
Reference List 119
Appendix C 112
   Article explaining Index Universal Life Insurance.
   By Todd Langford. Follow link to download article.

DEDICATION

I dedicate this book to those few clients who died early in my career. They gave me something no one else could have: the opportunity to deliver a death benefit check. It gave me a real sense of the responsibility I had in selling life insurance.

The whispers in my ear about life insurance came from God. Only a divine thought coming directly from God can give a man, for a few pennies a day, the ability to protect his wife and family from economic ruin if he was to die prematurely.

The insurance industry has lost a sense of the real importance of their products. They sell what they call competitive products for the benefit of the consumer. I propose that many are no better than car salesmen. Drive it awhile and trade it in so I can get a new sales commission. Life insurance is a lifetime product and should be purchased with a lifetime master plan in mind.

To Robert Castiglione, the creator and founder of LEAP Systems, Inc. Bob taught me about money and life insurance—the truth that was lost to marketing noise. I'd like to thank him for allowing me to use some of his quotes in this book and for his dedication to bringing truth about finance and insurance to the public.

To those clients who have lived and prospered because they believed in what I showed them about money and wealth creation and applied discipline to their financial lives. To the few I have coached who will amass a large amount of wealth in their lifetime; I salute you, for you prove that wealth is possible for all if they apply some basic rules, including discipline.

To Jody Victor, the master of business and personal growth. My wife and I have seen our lives change the most because of the influence of Jody and Kathy Victor.

Most of all, to my wife and daughter. They never stopped believing in me.

PREFACE

This book is intended to help you—the insurance buying public—move through the maze of protecting your family with the proper kind and amount of life insurance.

The insurance industry, for the most part, only cares about cash flow, premiums, and profits. The industry brings new products to the market according to what has sizzle and what will sell. These new products focus very little on the maximum benefit for the consumer.

When I joined the insurance industry in 1977, the marketplace was in the beginning stages of change. I was trained to sell people insurance based on the benefits, regardless of whether they lived or died.

Now only a small group of agents are trained to teach the consumer how to get the maximum use out of every dollar they spend.

Understanding universal life insurance is the most important element of this book. Universal life insurance is basically savings with term insurance. It is complex and has many moving parts that, if not monitored as to the interest rates and the premiums paid, could cause you to lose your life insurance and the premiums paid when you need the money most.

Term insurance is said to be the least expensive insurance to buy. I propose, however, that in many cases, it's the most expensive.

Before I dive into the more technical explanation relating to the various types of life insurance, let me share with you a story about the experience of a client, whose name has been changed for privacy purposes. Keep the story of Mr. Kelley in mind as you read the rest of the book. As you read, you will learn how to avoid the problems Mr. Kelley faced.

Mr. Kelley was a business owner in his early fifties. He decided to purchase real estate as an investment method. In the process of accumulating real estate, Mr. Kelly built up some large mortgages. So to protect himself and his assets, he decided to purchase a $500,000 universal life insurance policy with yearly premiums of about $3,250. This policy projected Mr. Kelley would have a huge cash value by age sixty-five.

Kelley was so excited about the potential benefits of this policy that he put an additional $125,000 into his policy during the first five years. The agent provided an illustration that predicted a higher than realistic interest rate. Expecting to pay a total premium of $147,000 during the first five years (based on the additional funds plus the $3,250 yearly premium), the policy illustrations projected a cash value of more than $460,000. See **illustration #9A** on pages 90-91.

Wisely, Kelley also bought a benefit called a waiver of premium, which guaranteed that the insurance company would pay the premium in his stead if he became disabled.

Unfortunately, Kelley was involved in an accident that left him permanently disabled. However, he still thought the policy would be okay because he had purchased the waiver of premium. What he didn't know was that the projected value of his policy was not guaranteed. The insurance company did continue to pay the annual premium of $3,250, but the extra money Kelley had planned to pay into his policy only reached $125,000.

Now the policy was scheduled to run out of cash by the time he was sixty-seven and would fall far short of the original $460,000 projection. To make matters worse, Kelley found out his policy would lapse in less than a year after I met with him, unless he paid $23,000 in added annual premiums. See **illustration #9B** on page 92.

Could the same thing happen to you that happened to Mr. Kelley? Sadly, yes.

"Many insurance agents are not exposed to the comprehensive education that would allow them to see that most products they market are inefficient in accomplishing what the client really wants."

It's true, sometimes these products do work. But if they don't, you had better beware. As a consumer, it is always in your best interest to be educated about the products to buy.

Think of it this way: Before you buy a car, you research for the best bargain, right? Wouldn't the best bargain be a car that is reliable, safe, and guaranteed to perform?

Now imagine that when the car is finally yours, the salesman tells you you're completely responsible for the vehicle's care, upkeep, and maintenance. As he ushers you out the door, he doesn't even give you the tools you need to perform these check-ups—not even directions or a manual. Opening the hood and being overwhelmed by all the parts and machinery is the same as buying a life insurance policy you don't understand without proper guidance from you agent.

The more you know, the safer your money is. Money is one of the most important things in life. In our society, we have to work to earn money to survive. Surveys show time and time again that most people hold wealth as one of the top three priorities in life. As people who must use money to survive, our finances are very precious to us. So, if this is true, why do so many people base the majority of their financial decisions on rumor, hearsay, and opinion?

You might believe you have been given sound financial advice, but in all likelihood, you have made the majority of your decisions based on advertisements and friends and family. Sometimes this works out well, but if the people you receive financial advice from are not fully informed about what they have invested in—which is often the case—you are almost completely blind as to what is happening with your money! Through my work, I have learned that most people spend more time and energy planning their vacations than they do their finances.

Why are people so uninformed about monetary decisions? I believe it is because most people don't really understand how these things work. Economics, finances, insurance, interest rates, banking, all of these are areas that we usually leave to the "experts." But what if these so called experts don't even have a full grasp of these concepts? There is a monumental responsibility that comes with handling wealth. Instead of trying to educate ourselves, we hand our money over to people we trust to understand finances, insurance, investments, etc., which can lead to some very tragic results.

In my years of experience, I have seen many people's lives completely changed for the worse by their lack of financial knowledge. I chose to write this book with the hope that the information I share here will help you avoid making bad choices that could eventually lead to financial ruin. The key to personal financial success and security lies in your hands.

The rest of this book is dedicated to helping you, the consumer, learn and understand more about the life insurance industry in order to make wise, sound, and beneficial choices regarding your finances. It is my sincere hope that through reading this book you will learn to avoid the problems that many of my customers have had to face and learn how to invest your money in ways that will give you the best return value.

"We cannot solve our current problems at the same level of thinking we were at when we created them!"

-Albert Einstein

"Success on any major scale requires you to accept responsibility... in the final analysis, the one quality that all successful people have... is the ability to take on responsibility."

-Michael Korda

Here's What People are Saying About Tom

Tom Young is MUCH MORE than a financial planner. His ethics are superb, and his standards are unparalleled by others in his field. He is honest, sincere, and genuinely cares about his clients. He shares his vast wealth of knowledge readily. He never uses pressure or force, but he consults and provides the guidance that enable us to make the best financial future that is secure, and that our investments are in the hands of the VERY BEST Certified Senior Advisor.

Stan and Mary Manecki
Retired Executive of Daimler Chrysler

We greatly appreciate the time you devoted to us recently. You have an extraordinary knowledge of economics and have unlocked the secret to moving money around to make it work. Thank you for having an interest in our financial well-being. It's clear to see that you do put people first.

G. Paich, Entrepreneur
Automotive Parts Store Owner

This book illustrates, demonstrates and teaches the flexibility and power of whole life insurance. Tom Young has clearly defined the risks associated with insurance products that outlive their owners, fall short of being fully funded, and in many cases, pass the financial risk on to the insured. This book could change the way you look at life insurance and your own personal financial planning.

Bruce Parker President, Global Life Business
Pan American Life Insurance Group

THE FAMILY MONEY FARM
WIDOWS AND ORPHANS
INTRODUCTION

Exodus 22:22-24 New International Version (NIV)
"Do not take advantage of the widow or the fatherless. If you do and they cry out to me, I will certainly hear their cry.

Every morning I crack open the newspaper and look at the obituaries while I have my coffee. Maybe it's a bit morbid, but sometimes I read the story of these people's lives, and I wonder, *How much wealth was lost because they were not insured to the maximum, or didn't have the right type of insurance, or because they took the wrong financial advice?*

Corporations like banks and insurance companies spend billions of dollars on marketing and advertising every day just to get you to think the way they want you to think. We get told how to act, what to do, and what to buy; we get bounced around like balls in a pinball machine. The average person isn't equipped to beat those kinds of odds. It isn't a fair fight. So I decided to write this book for the people behind those obituary stories—the widows and the orphans of the world. Because everyone is going to be either one or the other at least once in their lifetime. And if you don't change the way you think about money during your lifetime, you will always be at the mercy of the banks and corporations and so will the people you leave behind when you die.

I've been a CHFC (Charted Financial Consultant) for the last thirty years of my forty-year career, and I've spent nearly every day of my career disproving what I was taught by the financial world and helping my clients get control of their cash flow, avoid losses, and get out of debt in nine years or less. Sometimes I question how I got to this point in my life. Why do I think so differently? I took the same courses as everyone else took in my industry. How did I end up thinking the way that I think?

I truly believe in my heart that divine intervention had something to do with it because the experiences I've had led me in a completely different direction than I could have ever imagined.

Like most kids, I had an idol. Growing up, my dad had a friend named Tommy Johnson who was a mechanical engineer. Being from Kentucky, he always wore bib overalls, and you'd never guess it by looking at him, but he was the lead engineer at a local corporation and owned several patents on his own inventions. When I was ten years old, I wanted to grow up and be an engineer just like him. We all have people that set examples in our lives, whether we follow them or not, and I wanted to be a mechanical engineer like Mr. Johnson.

I didn't do great in high school. I wasn't stupid, but I had what I would call a demanding personality. My personality, which I understand better today because of my advanced certificate as a human behavior consultant, is a driver defiant personality. Of course, I didn't know that at the time. Now that I understand human personalities a bit better, I look back at that time, and I see that consistently, from my homework to my teachers, the more dominant someone was with me, the more defiant I was. It must have been in my blood because even my daughter inherited my personality traits. We butted heads a lot when she was growing up, but we are the best of friends today. You simply don't tell people like us what to do.

Despite my resistance to authority, somehow I graduated and went into the Air Force. Here was my big chance to be like my boyhood idol, Tommy Johnson. I was to be an aircraft jet engine mechanic. But life definitely had different plans for me because when they came back with the results of my placement exam, I got the second-highest score out of 10.

They said, "Look, you're too smart to be a mechanic." So, they made me a medic.

When I got out of the Air Force, I got married—to my wife of forty-nine years as of this writing—and I went to work as a laborer in a mill called American Bridge, then as a burner, and then as a welder. As I look back over the early days of my career, I realize I was dissatisfied with where I was in my life. I always wanted to be more and better, the best me I could be. One day, after I'd advanced as far as I was going to get in the mill, I left the mill to work on the railroad, where I was promised to be a foreman. But I soon left the railroad with dreams of going into business for myself. I decided to open an auto body shop. The auto body shop taught me the basics of business, but I still wasn't satisfied with this, so I sold my shop and went to work in a car dealership. A year later, after being ripped off by an insurance salesman, the manager offered me the opportunity to learn how to sell life insurance. That's when I found I had a taste for sales, and so naturally I got it into my head that I wanted to sell life insurance door to door.

I never went to college. I didn't even own a suit or a pair of dress pants. When I arrived at the Prudential Insurance Company office that day to take my twenty-eight question aptitude test, I sat right there in the office answering them one by one. I handed it back to my interviewer when I was done. I remember the look on his face when he handed it back to me. I thought I had failed. But he said, "How did you do that? You got all the questions right!"

He told me he'd been a manager for thirty years and had never had anyone get all the questions right.

Next, he handed me a three-ring binder, and I had to take a six-week training course. I took the binder home with me and did all six weeks in one. I stayed up until 2 A.M. every morning studying. I'd had all these dirty, grueling jobs—welding steel, stitching people up, working on cars—to me this was an opportunity of a lifetime. I wanted it to happen, and I would not be denied. Not only did I complete the course in one week, but I came in with a list of twice the number of initial prospects that was required of me. Because of my garage, I had written down two hundred names of customers from my business. I handed my new boss my list, and he said, "What's this?"

I simply said, "I did all six weeks. Here's my prospects."

He hired me on the spot, and I hadn't even passed the final exam yet. He said, "I have no doubt you will pass the test."

In a year I became the number one agent in that office and was promoted to sales manager. In ten months, our staff went from eighty-eighth out of ninety-five, to tenth in the region. I rose in ranks until I qualified for an international convention, but at a certain point, I started to feel resentful. I was out every night, plus Saturdays, and on top of it, managing all these lazy insurance agents. Here I was making all these people money, and none of them were even trying! I resigned from my management position and went back to being an agent. That year I ranked eighty-sixth out of twenty-five thousand agents. I just worked harder than anyone else.

Finally, I started my own insurance agency in January of 1980 so that I could be in a better position to offer independent advice and guidance to people. I worked contracts as a direct general agent, and

I did well for myself, but I was still hungry to learn more about the financial world. One day in the eighties, I met a man named Robert Castiglione. He created the LEAP system, which I was fascinated with. That system was the beginning of me learning about how money really works, and it changed my life completely. I was one of the first six people trained by Mr. Castiglione to do national training. I figured, if you want to really learn something, teach it. Because of the LEAP training, not only could I sell life insurance to my clients, I now had the materials and tools to really be able to help people manage their money—including myself.

Over the course of my career and training, I learned that most of what we were taught about finances are actually losing strategies. Unknowingly and unnecessarily, people lose millions over their lifetime, and what's worse is that they don't know they lost it or how to stop losing it. nobody tells us how to accumulate capital, how to avoid losses, or how to invest wisely. We think a certain way because we were told to think that way. We are told what to think, but we don't learn *how* to think, and because of this, everyone has some level of financial cancer. We've been indoctrinated by the government, corporations, and the banks. They've infected us with their thinking to get us to buy their products.

Most of the information we have all been taught and sold have been told to us by the salespeople of the world that want us to buy something. And I know this for a fact because I also fell victim to it. Like millions of other Americans, I didn't believe in delayed gratification. When I was young, and I wanted something, I went out and got it, and I buried my family in debt more than once. In the 1990s, I almost collapsed completely. I was on the edge of bankruptcy. I'm the biggest guy at fault. I didn't wake up to the way money really worked until I was in my forties. but at some point, I had to make a decision. I was either going to go over the falls, or I was going to learn how to step up to the plate and fix the mess I'd created. I chose to fix it.

You might have noticed that I have a lot of initials after my name. There's a reason for that. It's because I wanted to know the answer to the questions before I ask them. I took every financial certification course I could because I want to know how people are going to respond so I can help my clients get over themselves. Because we all need that. We need to get over ourselves.

So here I am today, I've been at this for over four decades, and I'm more excited today and have more passion for what I do than I have in the forty years up until today. I truly believe I have the answer and can teach people how to avoid financial cancer. Through this book, I'm going to change the way you think about money.

AUTHOR'S NOTE

This chapter of the book has been contributed by Dr. Robert A. Rohm, President of Personality Insights, Inc. from Atlanta, Georgia. The purpose of this chapter is to help the reader learn to more easily identify different personality styles. In this manner, productivity at work or in family relationships will increase.

Also, when doing financial planning, it is important to understand how personality styles affect the financial decision-making process. Some people are quick decision makers, while others are more cautious or reserved. Some are risk-takers, while others are less prone to step into untested waters. All of our financial decisions are greatly influenced by our own unique personality style. Therefore, it is of utmost importance that a person understands the Model of Human Behavior and how it relates to his or her decision-making process.

Although this book is primarily about life insurance and caring for loved ones after passing away, it is also a great idea to learn how to care for friends, associates, and loved ones while you are still alive! It is to that end that this chapter is affectionately dedicated. We hope you enjoy these powerful insights.

For further information, please feel free to visit Dr. Rohm's web site at www.personalityinsights.com.

FINDING YOUR STYLE

Years ago, scientists and philosophers began to recognize that the differences in people's behavior seemed to follow a pattern. They observed the personalities of people and described the behavior they saw. The D-I-S-C Model of Human Behavior is a result of their efforts. We can use it to increase our awareness and to understand why we think, feel, and act as we do.

Get the Picture...

Most people have predictable patterns of behavior—specific personality styles. There are four basic personality types, also known as temperaments. They blend together to determine your unique personality style. To help you understand why you often feel, think, and act the way you do, the following is a graphic overview of the Four Temperament Model of Human Behavior.

The four types are like four quarters of a circle. Before seeing the four parts as they stand alone, let's look at the circle in two parts. These two types are different from each other. Think of it this way: some people are more **outgoing**, while others are more **reserved**.

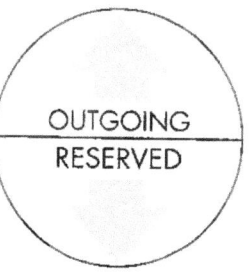

Outgoing people are more active and optimistic. **Reserved** types are more passive and pessimistic. One type is not better than the other. Both types of behavior are important.

Reserved types need to learn how to be more **dominant** and **inspiring**.

Outgoing people need to learn how to be more **supportive** and **cautious**.

There is another way to divide the circle. Two other types are also different from each other. You may recognize that some people are more **task-oriented**, while others are more **people-oriented**. Task-oriented types enjoy doing things (directing and correcting) while people-oriented individuals like to relate with others (**interacting** and **sharing**).

When you combine these two ways to divide the circle, you will see that they give the circle four parts, so you can visualize the four temperament types. **Everyone is a unique blend of these four parts.**

Let's Review

Outgoing people are more active and optimistic. Reserved people are more passive and cautious. One disposition is not better than the other. They are simply different, and both are important.

Outgoing People

There are several ways we can describe outgoing, fast-paced people. They love to go and do things. They seem to be excited or in a hurry most of the time. A crowd does not easily intimidate them because they love to be in the middle of whatever is happening! If a friend calls to ask, "Would you like to go to…," they have heard all they need to hear, and the answer is "Yes!" They thrive on doing many things at the same time. Rather than look for excitement, they create it. They don't have to go to the party; they are the party! They do not hesitate to jump into the pool of life feet first!

They are optimistic and positive. They look for the diamond in every lump of coal or the gold in every clump of dirt. They expect things to turn out well—or at least expect to be able to make things turn out well. Generally, they expect to win, and often they win with flair. Outward appearance and actions are usually more important to them than inward qualities and thoughts. They see the big picture and do not concentrate on details.

They are usually involved in community projects, civic clubs, church groups, and all kinds of organizations where they often hold leadership positions. They like being in charge of things, not because they do the most work, but because they like to tell others what to do! They are enthusiastic, so people like to put them in charge. When you eat a meal with these people, you may find that you are still enjoying your salad when they are asking for the dessert menu! They really believe that if a little is good, then more must be better! They have to learn that just enough may be just a little bit instead of a lot!

This type of person is energetic. They often plan to do more than they can do. They usually talk faster, work harder, and get others to help so they can get to their desired results in the end. They can echo the words of General George S. Patton, who said, "Lead me, follow me, or get out of my way!"

Reserved People

There are several ways to depict a person who is more reserved or slower-paced. They do not jump into the pool of life but prefer to test the waters first. After all, who knows how cold the water is? They simply hold back. They do not speak as freely or quickly as more outgoing individuals. However, this is not from a lack of interest. When they do speak, you will want to listen!

They may be like the proverbial tortoise who was left in the dust by the outgoing, fast-paced rabbit. But just like in the fable, they can cross the finish line ahead of those who started the race in a flash. They may be slower-paced, but they have patience and stamina to get the job done.

Reserved individuals are concerned about the details of a situation before doing something because they do not like to be surprised. They would prefer to have a safe plan rather than take things as they come. They are cautious and a little reluctant to get involved in too many activities. They tend to be more passive and content to watch the game instead of actually playing in it.

Reserved, or slower-paced, individuals are analytical and discerning. They concentrate on foundations and underlying details—not just on the big picture and outward appearances. These traits help them see the reality of a situation very quickly. To these people, quality and substance are important.

They prefer to operate behind the scenes by getting the job done and making sure everything is handled correctly. They have more difficulty starting a conversation with a stranger than a more outgoing person does, but what they share is worth the wait. They would rather have one or two close friends than have a crowd of acquaintances around them.

Your Motor Activity

Let's illustrate these two types of people. Each of us has an "internal motor" that drives us. It has a fast pace that makes us more outgoing, or it has a slow pace that makes us more reserved. In the illustrations below, we have divided our circle into two parts with a horizontal line. The arrows indicate that the darker shading, close to each tip, indicates more intensity in that trait, while the lighter shading, closer to the midline, shows less intensity in this motor activity. You may be extremely outgoing or reserved, or you may be just moderately outgoing or reserved. Remember, your personality style is also influenced by your environment. Therefore, depending upon your environment, at times you may be influenced to be more outgoing and at other times more reserved. For the sake of this illustration, however, just know that in general you tend to be either more outgoing or more reserved.

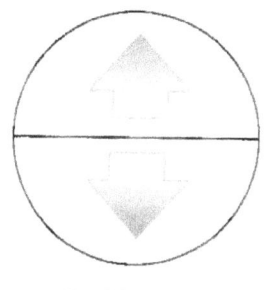

You have probably identified more closely with one side or the other of this circle. Regardless of which side of the circle is more comfortable for you, you can see that both types are valuable. They are different, and we need both types. We need outgoing, fast-paced people to get things going and get people excited. Although this is their natural approach, they can become aware of the need for balance in their own personality style and then learn how to be more steady and cautious. We need reserved, slower-paced people to take care of details and to be considerate of people. These reserved people can become aware of the need for balance in their own personality style and learn how to be more demanding and inspiring.

Are You Task-Oriented or People-Oriented?

We can also cut our circle into two parts the other way, vertically, representing two more distinct classifications of human personality. Some people are more task-oriented, while others are more people-oriented.

Task-oriented individuals enjoy doing things like making plans and working on projects. **People-oriented** individuals love to interact with other people and enjoy conversation while developing close friendships.

Task-Oriented People

Task-oriented people find great pleasure in a job well done. We like to call them high-tech. They focus on function. They like to make things work, so they love using technology. To this type, nothing is better than a fine-tuned, well-oiled, peak-performing machine. They talk about form and function. They want people and things to be in the best form and the best shape to perform the task at hand. They love online banking because they can access their balance at a moment's notice. They do not just talk about it, but they actually use this and other new forms of technology! They may still keep their own running balance in their head or on paper, but they love this form of convenience. They enjoy checking the bank and having access to their financial information at all times of the day or night.

These people are great at working on projects. They can really get into the process of seeing a job take shape and then watching it get accomplished. They are excellent planners who can see the end of a project from the beginning. They are the ones who put together plans that work! They agree with Ralph Waldo Emerson when he wrote, "What I must do is all that concerns me, not what the people think."

How might a task-oriented person approach a task? If you watch him rake his yard on a Saturday morning, you might observe him first coming out with a rake and looking the yard over like a field marshal preparing the battle plans. Then he rakes one section of the yard at a time, completing the job as efficiently as possible.

Imagine that his more people-oriented neighbor is out taking a nice, leisurely Saturday morning stroll. When the two friends see each other, the one who is raking the yard responds with a quick, "Hi!" However, he does not miss a stroke. He simply keeps raking as he secretly thinks, "Oh, no. I hope my neighbor doesn't stop to talk my ear off. I'm not out here to visit. I'm here to rake!" Should the unsuspecting neighbor continue to talk, he may find himself interrupted by his friend with the rake who says, "Excuse me; I'll be right back." Do you know where he is going? Yes, he is going into the garage to get another rake for his friend! He thinks to himself, "Two can rake better than one. If he wants to talk, I would be happy to listen, as long as I can get this job done." The task-oriented person also enjoys talking, but he has to get his work done. That is just the way he is wired.

People-Oriented People
Our people-oriented friends are very different. They are more interested in relationships with other people than in accomplishing a task. These people seem to be more emotional and more caring. They love talking and sharing feelings together. They just love to be with people. We like to call this side of the circle high-touch.

Imagine now that a neighbor needs to rake his yard. This person is more concerned about the feelings of other people, so he will handle the Saturday morning yard work very differently from a task-oriented person. Rather than being driven to complete the task, he will begin the project because he is concerned with what the neighbors might think if the yard looks bad. He feels compelled to rake the yard so that his neighbors will like him and be happy with him. He has a strong awareness of the needs and desires of people.

If someone walked by and stopped to talk to him while he was raking, he would smile and think, "This is great! I love talking with this neighbor!" Then he would probably say, "Why don't we go into the house, have a cup of coffee, and visit? I didn't want to rake the yard now, anyway! I can finish that later." Such is the nature of the people-oriented personality. Life is all about enjoying friendships with people.

Your Compass Activity

Let's illustrate this concept. Just as we have a motor that drives us, we also have a compass that draws us toward either tasks or people. Because we are drawn toward either tasks or people, we are either task-oriented or people-oriented. In the

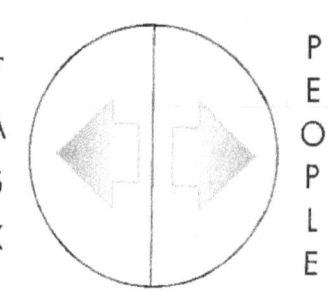

illustration to the right, the arrows indicate that the lighter shading, closer to the midline, shows less intensity in this compass activity, while the dark shading, towards each tip, reveals more intensity in each activity. You may be extremely people-oriented or task-oriented, or you may be just moderately people-oriented or task-oriented.

You have probably identified more closely with one or the other side of this circle. No matter which side of the circle is more comfortable for you, you can see that both types are valuable, and they are simply different. We need both types! We need task-oriented people to get our work planned and completed. Although this is their natural approach, they can become aware of the need for balance in their own personality style by learning how to be more conversational and to consider the feelings of others. We need people-oriented people to get everyone involved and to make each one feel more comfortable. They can become aware of the need for balance in their own personality style by learning how to plan their work and then work their plan.

Putting It All Together

When we put together both the motor activity of the outgoing and reserved types with the compass activity for the task and people-oriented types, we can see the four-quadrant Model of Human Behavior illustrated:

LIFE INSURANCE: WILL IT PAY WHEN I DIE?

We see that:
THE **D** TYPE IS OUTGOING AND TASK-ORIENTED
THE **I** TYPE IS OUTGOING AND PEOPLE-ORIENTED
THE **S** TYPE IS RESERVED AND PEOPLE-ORIENTED
THE **C** TYPE IS RESERVED AND TASK-ORIENTED

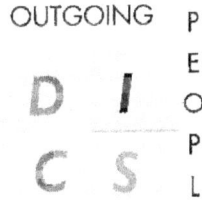

D Type

The **D** is in the top half of the circle, which is the **outgoing** half, and it is on the left side, which is the **task-oriented** side. Thus, the **D** type personality is **outgoing** and **task-oriented**.

I Type

The **I** is in the top half of the circle, which is the **outgoing** half, and it is on the right side, which is the **people-oriented** side. Thus, the **I** type personality is **outgoing** and **people-oriented**.

Both **D**s and **I**s are active and outgoing, but they go and do in different directions. The **D**, being **task-oriented**, has a strong desire to direct many people's activities to get a certain job completed. The **I**, being **people-oriented**, wants to look good in front of people. An **I** desires status and prestige.

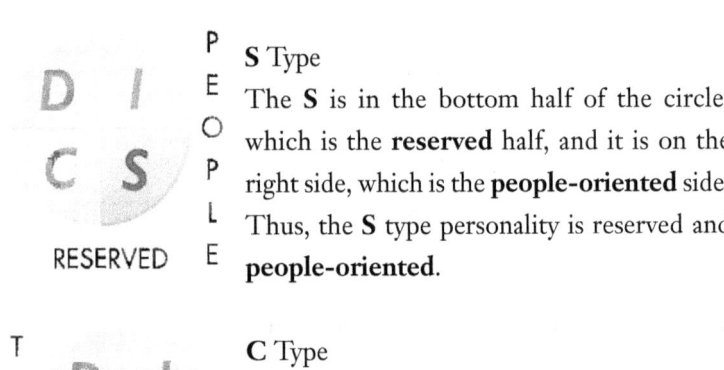

S Type

The **S** is in the bottom half of the circle, which is the **reserved** half, and it is on the right side, which is the **people-oriented** side. Thus, the **S** type personality is reserved and **people-oriented**.

C Type

The **C** is the bottom half of the circle, which is the **reserved** half, and it is on the left, which is the **task-oriented** side. Thus the **C** type personality is **reserved** and **task-oriented**.

Both **S**s and **C**s are reserved, but they have a different orientation. The **S**, being people-oriented, has a strong desire to please people and make everyone comfortable. The **C**, being task-oriented, wants to focus on his or her plans and procedures for getting the job done.

Remember, all four types have an important perspective to offer. One type isn't better than another. With this model, we are not looking for right and wrong or good and bad behavior. Each behavior type is important to consider in any situation. Each type has behavior that is effective and appropriate in some settings. We are exploring the differences in personality styles so that we can better understand ourselves and others.

What does DISC mean?

The letters in the four quadrants are significant because they are your keys to remembering the DISC Model of Human Behavior. As we look at these four quadrants of the circle together, we are able to visualize the DISC model. Each of us is a unique blend of these four parts. Let's introduce the symbol and explain the color for each **DISC** type now:

The **D** Type

We use an exclamation point to depict the **D** type because the **D** type is emphatic in everything! You will notice that the **D** is in the upper left quadrant of the circle. Green is our color for the **D** type because like a green light, it means GO! Six key traits, or characteristics, describe the outgoing and task-oriented **D** type: **D**ominant, **Di**rect, **D**emanding, **D**ecisive, **D**etermined and a **D**oer.

The **I** Type

We use a star to depict the **I** type, because the **I** type loves to be the star of the show! You will notice that the **I** is in the upper right quadrant of the circle. Red is our color for the **I** type, because it is fiery and exciting and shouts, "Stop and watch me!" Six key traits, or characteristics, describe the outgoing and people-oriented **I** type: **I**nspiring, **I**nfluencing, **I**mpressionable, **I**nteractive, **I**mpressive, and **I**nvolved.

The **S** Type

We use a plus or minus sign to depict the **S** type, because the **S** types are flexible and willing to respond, more or less, the way you might ask them to! You will notice that the **S** is in the lower right quadrant of the circle. Blue is our color for the **S** type because it is peaceful, harmonious color, just like the color of the sky. Six key traits, or characteristics, describe the reserved and people-oriented **S** type: **S**upportive, **S**table, **S**teady, **S**weet, **S**tatus quo and **S**hy.

? The **C** Type

We use a question mark to depict the **C** type, because the **C** type loves to question everything! You will notice that the **C** is in the lower left quadrant of the circle. Yellow is our color for the **C** type because it means caution, like the yellow in a traffic light. It also reminds us of the radiant energy of the sun, so it pictures the intensity of the **C** type. Six key traits, or characteristics, describe the reserved and task-oriented **C** type: Cautious, Calculating, Competent, Conscientious, Contemplative and Careful.

Getting the Keys

So far, we have presented the keys of the **DISC** Model of Human Behavior. You will see that each type is different, and each type is very special. As you think more about the traits of each type, you may be aware that you really identify most with one or two of these types.

Most people are predominantly strong in two or sometimes three types. However, you may only relate to just one of the traits, and, in addition to that, you may feel that you really do not understand one of the types at all. This is perfectly natural. We all have some of all four types within us. We usually have only one or two high (or strong) types, and one or two low (or weaker) types. The payoff for learning about our low types is invaluable because this is the place where we can learn to grow in the weak areas in our lives. Nevertheless, all this information gives you a great opportunity to learn about yourself and others.

You have a special personality style blend that includes characteristics, or traits, from all four classic **DISC** types.

You've got style!

PART I

CHAPTER ONE

WHAT IS LIFE INSURANCE?

The concept of life insurance dates back to before the Roman Empire. When the soldiers went out to battle, the sergeant collected pieces of gold for the families of men who didn't return. The soldiers' families shared in the amount collected. This was a basic form of insurance: the many sharing the cost of the loss of a few.

Life insurance is more than just the protection of economic responsibilities of a family, business, person, or entity. Life insurance should be the foundation to a financial plan.

We all recognize that we face an economic loss when our primary breadwinner dies, becomes disabled, or is otherwise unable to provide financial support for those who are financially dependent on them. Most of us feel that insurance is based on needs. However, life insurance protection is unlike other forms of insurance, such as homeowner, fire, or casualty and liability insurance. These products relate to replacement cost or economic value. Life insurance protects human life value, not just some stated need.

If you are insured properly, with coverage equal to your human life value, all your needs will be covered. The needs approach to selling life insurance was a sales idea conceived by the insurance industry to help the production of new salespeople with little insurance or financial education.

The American College, founded in 1927 by Solomon Heubner, was expected to be the education institution that would bring professionalism to the sale of life insurance.

Heubner invented this concept that the proper amount of life insurance should be measured in human life value. He also said, "There is no one royal road—one blanket formula—for such appraisals."

Most insurance companies today use a multiple of annual income to determine how much insurance the consumer should buy.

A man thirty years old can buy approximately twenty-five times his annual earnings. A man of fifty might buy fifteen or twenty times his earnings. Someone with a sizable estate can buy life insurance equal to the value of that estate. It is not an easy calculation, and, therefore, most people are grossly underinsured.

The perceived premium cost is the primary factor that prevents people from buying the proper amount of life insurance.

I will continue to cover some of the methods that will allow you to become properly insured. If you are interested in talking about your personal financial situation, feel free to call me 724-728-6820 or email thomasyoung@1stconsultantsinc.com or visit www.1stconsultantsinc.com.

CHAPTER TWO

SOME HISTORY OF THE LIFE INSURANCE INDUSTRY

For the most part, life insurance was introduced in America in the 1800's. Around 1950, the industry as a whole was marred by fraud and mismanagement. The Armstrong investigation, which took place in New York, centered on misuse of policyholders' money and insurance companies not paying claims on the most common type of insurance in this era, accessible life.

Accessible life allowed the insurance company to adjust the premium based on company expenses and claims, much like some modern insurances. However, the practices of accessible life sent expenses out of control. Making a claim was a terrifying process. Insurable interest, or the condition that the policyholder or beneficiary had to have an economic risk if the insured died, was non-existent. Accessible life was basically like buying insurance on people you don't know and collecting when they die. Surely you can see how that would cause a problem for some people. Sound familiar? A similar concept made headlines recently when companies were caught buying insurance on their employees to collect the benefits.

Ask yourself, why do financial institutions sell us these products? Do they sell them to us to do us a favor, to help us protect ourselves, or to make a profit?

When products are recommended for purchase, we need some basic understanding of the game to make an informed decision. What products are in our best interest and which are not? Let's see how things have changed over the last thirty years or so.

"We never know the wealth of water 'till the well runs dry."
-English Proverb

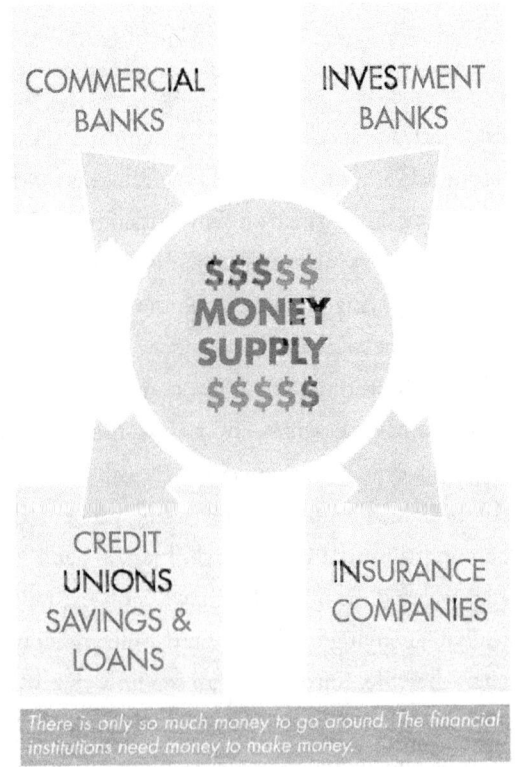

Illustration #1

Most financial products available today are sold in reaction to government regulations involving products created by competitive financial institutions that want to control the lifeblood of their profits and money supply.

Commercial banks, investment banks, insurance companies, credit unions, and savings and loans are in the business of making money. If there was no profit in it for them, do you really think they would lend you money? The first quarter of 2003 was the most profitable time in banking history.

Let me share a story about money and politics. In the late 1980s, interest rates were still very high after peaking at 25 percent. The savings and loans were collapsing around us, and the government was telling us the bailout could cost as much as $250 billion.

Recognizing this problem, Paul Zane Pilzer gave a presentation to Congress in 1985 about the pending collapse of the savings and loans. Unfortunately, Congress didn't buy Pilzer's theory. A couple years later, after ignoring his warnings and recommendations, the savings and loans defaulted. Pilzer later published his book called *Other Peoples Money*, containing the notes he had presented to Congress.

Since they were closely related, logic told us that if the savings and loans were defunct, the banks could not be far behind.

The banks' demise began around 1970 when widespread deregulation began. Banks were not legally permitted to pay interest on checking accounts. So, a small northeastern bank decided to offer checks with a savings account. Thus, new financial tools called "now accounts" and "super now accounts" were born.

Eventually, banks and savings and loans were on the same financial plane. Mortgages that were only available from savings and loans also became available through banks. If savings and loans were in trouble by the mid-1980s, the banks could be expected to follow right behind. Who could fix the problem?

In the early 1990s, the Federal Reserve, headed by Alan Greenspan, was faced with the expectation that the failure of three banks would bankrupt the FDIC. The Federal Reserve board, under Greenspan's leadership, had to create a plan to save the banks from collapse (The Federal Reserve sets the rules regarding velocity of money and the multiplier effect and sets monetary policy for the banking system).

Consider this scenario. It's 1991, and you are a borrower. The banks would loan you money at 15 percent interest. If you were a saver, the bank would pay you 9 percent interest on your certificate of deposit (CD). The banks would see a 6 percent gross profit; that is a 66 2/3 profit.

Two years later, the rates had come down. America was in a recession. The interest rates had fallen to the point where a CD only paid 3 percent, but you could borrow money for as low as 9 percent. That is still a 6 percent profit margin. That is 9 percent for the bank versus 3 percent for you. That, my friend, is a 200 percent profit margin. I guess the headlines in the major news sources said it best: the years 1992 through 1995 were the most profitable years in banking history.

```
15% loan rate = Gross earnings to bank
-9% CD interest = What banks pay for use of your money
6% Gross Profit
6% / 9% = 66 2/3% profit
                    VS
9% loan rate = Gross earnings to bank
-3% CD interest = What banks pay for use of your money
6% Gross Profit
6% / 3% = 200% profit
```

Illustration 2

Refer back to **illustration #1** on page 38 and let me share with you more history. It was 1970, and the banks won the right to pay interest on checking accounts. This moved more money control to the banks. In 1972, the life insurance industry created the flexible premium annuity. This allowed flexible premium deposits into a tax-deferred product. The kicker was, you could withdraw 10 percent per year tax free. At the end of ten years, you got your money back, and the interest was sheltered from taxes. The life insurance industry now had a powerful array of tax-favored products, including whole life insurance with dividends from participating life insurance companies.

Participating whole life insurance has a rate of return sometimes equivalent to 3 percent to 6 percent in a bank account over a lifetime, thus rendering the life insurance costless.

With participating whole life, you could borrow at a 1 to 3 percent net cost without being taxed. You could surrender dividends and pay no tax until you got all your original payments back. The law being followed was referred to as FIFO, or "First In First Out." The first money in was your premium, and until you got all the premiums back, there was no tax. The power of the participating whole life plan made the other players jealous. The other sellers had a hard time competing for money against this type of insurance.

In 1977, E.F. Hutton created a product called universal life insurance. This was marketed as the company's answer to what it felt was a big insurance rip off. Almost all the marketing for universal life was focused on the overpriced cost of whole life. Thus, the consumer was supposed to believe it had to be a rip off.

This marketing campaign was the biggest I had seen in my twenty-seven years in the insurance business. It created a firestorm that led to wholesale replacement of good insurance. People were led to believe this was the unbundling of whole life insurance, and the message was that the insurance industry was overcharging the public with expensive whole life insurance.

The first versions of universal life were comprised of all savings and very little life insurance. They guaranteed the principal at 6 percent, like a CD, and tacked on the minimum amount of life insurance. For example, a one hundred thousand dollar deposit paid a five thousand dollar death benefit. The interest would be guaranteed for maybe a year at 6 percent, and this was all wrapped up in a life insurance policy that had favorable tax treatment. This product also allowed you to withdraw or borrow to access your money and still pay no tax. When the insured died, the load was paid from the tax-free death benefit, and there was still no income tax due.

When the interest rates started to rise in the eighties, universal life became a big threat to the traditional life insurance companies that sold participating whole life. They were threatened by disintermediation—cash surrendering of the policies or borrowing the money at 4 or 5 percent and getting 10 percent, 12 percent, or more interest, causing a run on the bank).

The companies that sold participating whole life felt so threatened that instead of educating their policyholders about the great benefits they had in their policies, they started to replace their own policies with universal life. Consumers were told universal life was the new product and that they should switch one for the other. I saw agents win awards for sales achievement when all they did was make their companies richer with no benefit to the consumer.

I believe this was the greatest disservice to the American public ever. The companies were actually using the popularity of this new, misleading product to relieve themselves of their fiduciary responsibility. The cash value in whole life is sacred because it backs the guarantees. However, the cash value of universal life is a bucket of cash at the insurance companies' disposal.

In 1984, the TAMRA Act changed the way these products were taxed. Regulators felt the new products gave insurance companies too much tax advantage, so they used their influence through political action committees and recommended new laws to be enacted. One of those laws was the TAMRA Act, which changed the rules involving universal life. The mandated premium guidelines and modified endowment contract (MEC) rules meant that now there was a limit to the premium you could pay in relation to the amount of death benefit the policy would pay. This, in most regards, killed universal life's value to consumers.

But the plan backfired. The insurance companies figured out a way to make it the most profitable insurance policy ever. They saw it as the ultimate "buy term and invest the difference" product, a concept espoused by A.L. Williams Company. The problem is, many of these companies have been sued for non-disclosure of non-guarantees and for churning in this type of insurance.

The replacement of insurance was supposed to be monitored by the insurance companies, which failed miserably to uphold their fiduciary responsibility toward the consumer. I only realized this failure when I became involved in a movement to bring truth to the public by teaching them about the efficiencies for money relating to the economics of creating wealth.

As I hope I have helped you understand, the truth is that most products today are not in your best interest but are designed to be in the best interest of the insurance companies. Most agents are honest but misinformed as to the truth and purpose of life insurance. Some are too wrapped up in the commissions.

Remember: "Opinion is fact until challenged."

Many times, a new product has too many advantages. The government steps in after the market is saturated, and the public doesn't know the rules and benefits have changed. Agents see the new product design as a way to recommend replacement of older policies with some new product that's better.

The focus should always be on making the current product work for the client. Only when all other options are exhausted would a replacement insurance product be appropriate. Replacement, for the most part, is a new commission for the sales agent and a new cost for you, the buyer. You should understand all the ramifications of the new product before buying. Whatever you buy as a replacement product must move you forward toward your goals.

I always ask my clients why they bought the $25,000 or $50,000 face amount instead of another amount. You must ask yourself what economic evaluation process did the agent use to determine the face amount purchased? Was it just his goal to sell you that much? We don't live in even amounts, so why should we receive a nice round value for our lives?

If you purchased a universal life insurance policy, ask the insurance company for an inforce illustration. That will give you a look at the present performance of the policy. You must keep the goals of the policy in mind (See the Life Insurance Goal Planning worksheet in **Exhibit #2** on pages 127, 128 and 129.) The new projection should show you what adjustments you have to increase your premium payments to make up for lost interest or increased morality costs.

I believe an insurance company should automatically send clients an illustration each year to show where premium payment adjustments are needed to meet the goals of the policy.

When you buy a universal life insurance policy, there should be a statement of purpose as to what they expect the policy to provide. Once this is set, the insurance company should run an inforce illustration, targeting whatever results the client anticipates. This would show you where you need to pay more premium to meet that goal due to ongoing variables in the policy, such as interest rates and morality charge changes. I think this would solve many of the misconceptions about universal life. If you don't want the risk of having to pay more, maybe you would discover this isn't the right kind of insurance for the goal before purchasing the policy.

CHAPTER THREE

UNIVERSAL LIFE INSURANCE

VUL

IUL

E.F. Hutton was the first company to introduce universal life insurance. It became the competitive alternative to participating whole life and in turn became the replacement product for many agents. It was used to replace good, permanent whole life types of insurance.

By the early 1980s, agents were using computer illustrations to show prospects a lower premium for the same insurance amount or the same premium for a larger amount of insurance. These illustrations often projected high interest rates far into the future, which was logically impossible. The basis for the product was a savings fund and an insurance element. People were led to believe that interest rates on the savings element were going to be high for many years into the future and the emphasis on the minimum interest was avoided since it would show a deficiency of premiums. Who would be interested in getting more life insurance for the same premium cost or a lower premium for the same amount of insurance?

> **Illustration 3** on pages 48 - 49 is an example of a *universal life policy* illustrating the minimum premium. As you can see, the policy terminates in year 19 under the guarantees and year 28 for the current assumptions.
>
> **Illustrations 4A and 4B** on pages 50 to 53 are based on what is called the *target premium*, which is usually the commissionable premium or the amount of premium at which the agent's commission is calculated. It terminates under the guarantees in year 29 and the current rate keeps it going to the 43rd year, or to age 88. Remember that these illustrations are projections and are not guaranteed.

THOMAS W. YOUNG

Flexible Premium Adjustable Life Insurance

Designed For: **Tom Young** / Male/ Age 45 / Non-Tobacco

Policy values are based on the policy, riders and benefits shown in the Narrative Summary. All premiums are assumed to be paid out-of-pocket. No loans or partial surrenders are taken from policy.

End of Year	Age	Annualized Premium Outlay	Guaranteed Values	
			Policy Account Value	Cash Surrender Value
1	46	720	412	0
2	47	720	815	0
3	48	720	1,206	0
4	49	720	1,583	0
5	50	720	1,941	0
6	51	720	2,279	0
7	52	720	2,588	0
8	53	720	2,860	64
9	54	720	3,089	354
10	55	720	3,262	588
11	56		3,372	1,233
12	57	720	3,406	1,802
13	58	720	3,356	2,287
14	59	720	3,212	2,678
15	60	720	2,955	2,955
16	61		2,567	2,567
17	62	720	2,028	2,028
18	63	720	1,308	1,308
19	64	720	373	373
20	65	720	Lapsed	Lapsed
21	66	720	Lapsed	Lapsed
22	67	720	Lapsed	Lapsed
23	68	720	Lapsed	Lapsed
24	69	720	Lapsed	Lapsed
25	70	720	Lapsed	Lapsed
26	71	720	Lapsed	Lapsed
27	72	720	Lapsed	Lapsed
28	73	720	Lapsed	Lapsed
29	74	*	Lapsed	Lapsed

	Guaranteed	
	10 Year	20 Year
Surrender Cost Index:	6.75	N/A
Net Payment Index:	7.20	N/A

48

LIFE INSURANCE: WILL IT PAY WHEN I DIE?

Basic Illustration

Illustration 3

Initial Specified Amount = $100,000.00
Initial Death Benefit Option = Level (Option A)
Planned Premium = $720.00
Premium Mode = Annual

Guaranteed Values	Total Values Including Non-Guaranteed Assumptions*		
Death Benefit	Policy Account Value	Cash Surrender Value	Death Benefit
100,000	413	0	100,000
100,000	816	0	100,000
100,000	1,208	0	100,000
100,000	1,586	0	100,000
100,000	1,946	0	100,000
100,000	2,285	0	100,000
100,000	2,595	0	100,000
100,000	2,873	77	100,000
100,000	3,102	367	100,000
100,000	3,277	603	100,000
100,000	3,843	1,704	100,000
100,000	4,382	2,778	100,000
100,000	4,876	3,807	100,000
100,000	5,320	4,786	100,000
100,000	5,701	5,701	100,000
100,000	6,066	6,006	100,000
100,000	6,230	6,230	100,000
100,000	6,359	6,359	100,000
100,000	6,380	6,380	100,000
Lapsed	6,276	6,276	100,000
Lapsed	6,171	6,171	100,000
Lapsed	5,943	5,943	100,000
Lapsed	5,574	5,574	100,000
Lapsed	5,042	5,042	100,000
Lapsed	4,323	4,323	100,000
Lapsed	3,413	3,413	100,000
Lapsed	2,289	2,289	100,000
Lapsed	929	929	100,000
Lapsed	Lapsed	Lapsed	Lapsed

Assumed

10 Year	20 Year
6.74	5.39
7.20	7.20

* These values are based on the Current Interest Rate of 4.00% and the Current Monthly Deductions.

THOMAS W. YOUNG

Flexible Premium Adjustable Life Insurance

Designed For: **Tom Young** / Male/ Age 45 / Non-Tobacco

Policy values are based on the policy, riders and benefits shown in the Narrative Summary. All premiums are assumed to be paid out-of-pocket. No loans or partial surrenders are taken from policy.

			Guaranteed Values	
End of Year	Age	Annualized Premium Outlay	Policy Account Value	Cash Surrender Value
1	46	1,135	845	0
2	47	1,135	1,700	0
3	48	1,135	2,563	0
4	49	1,135	3,434	408
5	50	1,135	4,309	1,339
6	51	1,135	5,187	2,274
7	52	1,135	6,063	3,208
8	53	1,135	6,929	4,133
9	54	1,135	7,782	5,047
10	55	1,135	8,613	5,939
11	56	1,135	9,415	7,276
12	57	1,135	10,181	8,577
13	58	1,135	10,906	9,837
14	59	1,135	11,583	11,049
15	60	1,135	12,198	12,198
16	61	1,135	12,740	12,740
17	62	1,135	13,195	13,195
18	63	1,135	13,542	13,542
19	64	1,135	13,757	13,757
20	65	1,135	13,814	13,814
21	66	1,135	13,684	13,684
22	67	1,135	13,341	13,341
23	68	1,135	12,752	12,752
24	69	1,135	11,878	11,878
25	70	1,135	10,673	10,673
26	71	1,135	9,068	9,068
27	72	1,135	6,918	6,918
28	73	1,135	4,221	4,221
29	74	1,135	776	776
30	75	1,135	Lapsed	Lapsed
31	76	1,135	Lapsed	Lapsed
32	77	1,135	Lapsed	Lapsed
33	78	1,135	Lapsed	Lapsed
34	79	1,135	Lapsed	Lapsed
35	80	1,135	Lapsed	Lapsed

LIFE INSURANCE: WILL IT PAY WHEN I DIE?

Basic Illustration

Illustration 4A

Initial Specified Amount = $100,000.00
Initial Death Benefit Option = Level (Option A)
Planned Premium = $ 1,135 .00
Premium Mode = Annual

Guaranteed Values	Total Values Including Non-Guaranteed Assumptions*		
Death Benefit	Policy Account Value	Cash Surrender Value	Death Benefit
100,000	846	0	100,000
100,000	1,701	0	100,000
100,000	2,565	0	100,000
100,000	3,437	411	100,000
100,000	4,313	1,343	100,000
100,000	5,192	2,279	100,000
100,000	6,069	3,214	100,000
100,000	6,942	4,146	100,000
100,000	7,795	5,060	100,000
100,000	8,627	5,953	100,000
100,000	9,858	7,719	100,000
100,000	11,094	9,490	100,000
100,000	12,322	11,253	100,000
100,000	13,537	13,003	100,000
100,000	14,733	14,733	100,000
100,000	15,901	15,901	100,000
100,000	17,038	17,038	100,000
100,000	18,139	18,139	100,000
100,000	19,194	19,194	100,000
100,000	20,196	20,196	100,000
100,000	21,254	21,254	100,000
100,000	22,269	22,269	100,000
100,000	23,233	23,233	100,000
100,000	24,136	24,136	100,000
100,000	24,966	24,966	100,000
100,000	25,728	25,728	100,000
100,000	26,416	26,416	100,000
100,000	27,021	27,021	100,000
100,000	27,533	27,533	100,000
Lapsed	28,023	28,023	100,000
Lapsed	28,482	28,428	100,000
Lapsed	28,768	28,768	100,000
Lapsed	28,848	28,848	100,000
Lapsed	28,683	28,683	100,000
Lapsed	28,227	28,277	100,000

Flexible Premium Adjustable Life Insurance

End of Year	Age	Annualized Premium Outlay	Guaranteed Values	
			Policy Account Value	Cash Surrender Value
36	81	1,135	Lapsed	Lapsed
37	82	1,135	Lapsed	Lapsed
38	83	1,135	Lapsed	Lapsed
39	84	1,135	Lapsed	Lapsed
40	85	1,135	Lapsed	Lapsed
41	86	1,135	Lapsed	Lapsed
42	87	1,135	Lapsed	Lapsed
43	88	1,135	Lapsed	Lapsed
44	89	*	Lapsed	Lapsed

	Guaranteed	
	10 Year	20 Year
Surrender Cost Index:	6.85	7.37
Net Payment Index:	11.5	11.35

Continue   **Illustration 4B**

Guaranteed Values	Total Values Including **Non-Guaranteed Assumptions***		
Death Benefit	Policy Account Value	Cash Surrender Value	Death Benefit
Lapsed	27,430	27,430	100,000
Lapsed	26,232	26,232	100,000
Lapsed	24,559	24,559	100,000
Lapsed	22,322	22,322	100,000
Lapsed	19,394	19,394	100,000
Lapsed	15,894	15,892	100,000
Lapsed	11,409	11,409	100,000
Lapsed	5,708	5,708	100,000
Lapsed	Lapsed	Lapsed	Lapsed

Assumed

10 Year	20 Year
6.84	5.53
11.35	11.35

* These values are based on the Current Interest Rate of 4.00% and the Current Monthly Deductions.

Illustrations 5 A and 5B on pages 54 - 57 shows a maximum premium that is close to what a whole life premium would be. It appears that it would last to age 95. The death benefit would be much higher on the participating whole life policy. When does the face amount begin to increase compared to participating Whole Life on page 58 - 61?

Flexible Premium Adjustable Life Insurance

Designed For: **Tom Young** / Male / Age 45 / Non-Tobacco

Policy values are based on the policy, riders and benefits shown in the Narrative Summary. All premiums are assumed to be paid out-of-pocket. No loans or partial surrenders are taken from policy.

End of Year	Age	Annualized Premium Outlay	Guaranteed Values	
			Policy Account Value	Cash Surrender Value
1	46	2,020	1,769	920
2	47	2,020	3,587	1,878
3	48	2,020	5,456	2,873
4	49	2,020	7,381	4,355
5	50	2,020	9,357	6,387
6	51	2,020	11,389	8,475
7	52	2,020	13,473	10,617
8	53	2,020	15,607	12,811
9	54	2,020	17,791	15,056
10	55	2,020	20,024	17,350
11	56	121	20,314	18,175
12	57	1,710	22,217	20,603
13	58	1,836	24,179	23,210
14	59	1,836	26,373	25,870
15	60	1,836	28,496	28,496
16	61	1,836	30,646	30,645
17	62	1,836	32,810	32,819
18	63	1,836	35,011	35,011
19	64	1,836	37,215	37,215
20	65	1,836	39,426	39,425
21	66	1,836	41,641	42,641
22	67	1,836	43,860	43,860
23	68	1,836	46,082	46,082
24	69	1,836	48,305	48,309
25	70	1,836	50,541	50,541
26	71	1,836	52,773	52,773
27	72	1,836	54,970	54,470
28	73	1,836	57,177	57,177
29	74	1,836	59,550	59,159
30	75	1,836	61,508	61,308
31	76	1,836	63,631	63,631
32	77	1,836	65,736	65,736
33	78	1,836	67,839	67,839
34	79	1,836	69,960	69,960
35	80	1,836	72,119	72,119

Basic Illustration

Illustration 5A

Initial Specified Amount = $100,000.00
Initial Death Benefit Option = Level (Option A)
Planned Premium = $ 1,135 .00
Premium Mode = Annual

Guaranteed Values	Total Values Including Non-Guaranteed Assumptions*		
Death Benefit	Policy Account Value	Cash Surrender Value	Death Benefit
100,000	1,749	920	100,000
100,000	3,589	1,878	100,000
100,000	5,460	2,873	100,000
100,000	7,384	4,358	100,000
100,000	9,362	6,392	100,000
100,000	11,794	8,481	100,000
100,000	13,479	10,624	100,000
100,000	15,018	12,822	100,000
100,000	17,804	15,069	100,000
100,000	20,037	17,363	100,000
100,000	20,705	18,566	100,000
100,000	23,017	21,413	100,000
100,000	25,509	24,440	100,000
100,000	27,456	27,522	100,000
100,000	30,658	30,058	100,000
100,000	33,312	33,513	100,000
100,000	36,028	36,028	100,000
100,000	38,805	38,805	100,000
100,000	41,647	41,647	100,000
100,000	44,559	44,559	100,000
100,000	47,624	47,624	100,000
100,000	50,787	50,787	100,000
100,000	54,253	54,055	100,000
100,000	57,437	57,437	100,000
100,000	60,941	60,944	100,000
100,000	64,509	64,599	100,000
100,000	68,417	68,417	100,000
100,000	72,422	72,422	100,000
100,000	76,635	76,035	100,000
100,000	81,107	81,107	100,000
100,000	85,859	83,859	100,000
100,000	90,899	90,199	100,000
100,000	96,269	96,269	101,043
100,000	101,864	101,864	106,957
100,000	107,654	107,654	113,037

Flexible Premium Adjustable Life Insurance

End of Year	Age	Annualized Premium Outlay	Guaranteed Values	
			Policy Account Value	Cash Surrender Value
36	81	1,836	74,335	74,335
37	82	1,836	76,632	76,622
38	83	1,836	79,039	79,039
39	84	1,836	81,602	81,502
40	85	1,836	84,397	84,347
41	86	1,836	87,544	87,544
42	87	1,836	91,220	91,220
43	88	1,836	95,678	95,678
44	89	1,836	100,410	100,410
45	90	1,836	105,193	105,193
46	91	1,836	110,014	110,014
47	92	1,836	115,171	115,171
48	93	1,836	120,734	120,734
49	94	1,836	126,792	126,792
50	95	1,836	133,455	133,455

	Guaranteed	
	10 Year	20 Year
Surrender Cost Index:	7.06	7.28
Net Payment Index:	20.20	18.64

LIFE INSURANCE: WILL IT PAY WHEN I DIE?

Continue   **Illustration 5B**

Guaranteed Values	Total Values Including Non-Guaranteed Assumptions*		
Death Benefit	Policy Account Value	Cash Surrender Value	Death Benefit
100,000	113,643	113,643	113,643
100,000	119,835	119,825	119,825
100,000	126,232	126,232	126,232
100,000	132,857	132,837	132,837
100,000	139,651	139,651	139,651
100,000	146,696	146,696	146,696
100,000	153,953	153,953	153,953
100,462	161,421	161,421	161,421
105,431	169,097	169,097	169,097
110,432	176,979	176,929	176,929
115,515	185,064	185,064	185,064
119,778	193,568	193,568	193,568
124,356	202,553	202,553	202,553
129,328	212,091	212,091	212,091
132,789	222,270	223,270	223,270

Assumed

10 Year	20 Year
7.05	5.80
20.20	18.64

* These values are based on the Current Interest Rate of 4.00% and the Current Monthly Deductions.

THOMAS W. YOUNG

Illustrations 6A and 6B on pages 58 - 61 shows a whole life policy. I invite you to compare the numbers yourself.

Level Premium Whole Life Insurance Paid Up at

Designed For: **Tom Young** / Male / Age 45 / Non-Tobacco

Policy values are based on the policy, riders and benefits shown in the Narrative Summary. All premiums are assumed to be paid out-of-pocket. No loans or partial surrenders are taken from policy.

			Guaranteed Values	
End of Year	Age	Annualized Contract Premium	Cash Surrender Value	Death Benefit
1	46	2,060	0	100,000
2	47	2,060	808	100,000
3	48	2,060	2,752	100,000
4	49	2,060	4,754	100,000
5	50	2,060	6,812	100,000
6	51	2,060	8,608	100,000
7	52	2,060	10,443	100,000
8	53	2,060	12,314	100,000
9	54	2,060	14,218	100,000
10	55	2,060	16,150	100,000
11	56	2,060	18,110	100,000
12	57	2,060	20,097	100,000
13	58	2,060	22,119	100,000
14	59	2,060	24,158	100,000
15	60	2,060	26,735	100,000
16	61	2,060	28,333	100,000
17	62	2,060	30,454	100,000
18	63	2,060	32,585	100,000
19	64	2,060	34,744	100,000
20	65	2,060	36,896	100,000
21	66	1,938	39,049	100,000
22	67	1,938	41,102	100,000
23	68	1,938	43,358	100,000
24	69	1,938	45,517	100,000
25	70	1,938	47,679	100,000
26	71	1,938	49,694	100,000
27	72	1,938	51,912	100,000
28	73	1,938	54,105	100,000
29	74	1,938	56,186	100,000
30	75	1,938	58,217	100,000
31	76	1,938	60,196	100,000
32	77	1,938	62,127	100,000
33	78	1,938	64,020	100,000
34	79	1,938	65,888	100,000
35	80	1,938	67,742	100,000

Age 90

Basic Illustration

Illustration 6A

Initial Specified Amount = $100,000.00
Total Initial Annual Premium = $2,060.00
Premium Mode = Annual
Dividend Option = Paid Up Additions

Total Values Including Non-Guaranteed Assumptions*

Annual Dividend	Cash Surrender Value	Death Benefit
0	0	100,000
40	848	100,121
55	2,848	100,280
72	4,926	100,484
100	7,089	100,756
145	9,039	101,138
209	11,098	101,674
281	13,271	102,371
353	15,559	103,219
431	17,965	104,222
497	20,478	105,344
554	23,091	106,558
611	25,808	107,857
669	28,630	109,240
746	31,581	110,738
832	34,666	112,361
933	37,900	114,134
1,042	41,286	116,060
1,165	44,833	118,156
1,298	48,546	120,432
1,441	52,437	122,896
1,585	56,508	125,540
1,730	60,765	128,359
1,870	65,207	131,335
2,028	69,853	134,489
2,217	74,729	137,862
2,425	79,846	141,471
2,659	85,215	145,348
2,915	90,842	149,513
3,182	96,725	153,973
3,429	102,841	158,693
3,690	109,210	163,684
3,941	115,833	168,927
4,185	122,723	174,406
4,436	129,900	180,124

Level Premium Whole Life Insurance Paid Up at

End of Year	Age	Annualized Contract Premium	Guaranteed Values	
			Cash Surrender Value	Death Benefit
36	81	1,938	69,584	100,000
37	82	1,938	71,415	100,000
38	83	1,938	73,229	100,000
39	84	1,938	75,029	100,000
40	85	1,938	76,813	100,000
41	86	1,938	79,623	100,000
42	87	1,938	80,504	100,000
43	88	1,938	82,520	100,000
44	89	1,938	84,782	100,000
45	90	1,938	87,437	100,000
46	91	0	88,270	100,000
47	92	0	89,148	100,000
48	93	0	90,078	100,000
49	94	0	91,102	100,000
50	95	0	92,250	100,000
51	96	0	93,525	100,000
52	97	0	94,022	100,000
53	98	0	96,400	100,000
54	99	0	97,816	100,000
55	100	0	100,000	100,000

	Guaranteed	
	10 Year	20 Year
Surrender Cost Index:	7.15	8.75
Net Payment Index:	19.38	19.38

Age 90

Illustration 6B

Total Values Including Non-Guaranteed Assumptions*

Annual Dividend	Cash Surrender Value	Death Benefit
4,709	137,389	186,104
5,003	145,206	192,366
5,332	153,372	198,949
5,695	161,908	205,889
6,057	170,814	213,182
6,415	180,113	220,819
6,762	189,842	228,783
7,081	200,054	237,039
7,366	210,834	245,544
7,616	222,313	254,255
7,672	232,118	262,946
7,902	242,312	271,810
7,824	252,665	280,496
7,675	263,215	288,921
7,457	273,983	297,005
7,459	285,240	304,980
7,565	297,064	312,949
7,736	309,398	320,975
7,832	321,797	328,982
5,438	334,420	334,420

Assumed

10 Year	20 Year
5.28	4.02
17.51	14.65

* These values are based on the Current Interest Rate of 4.00% and the Current Monthly Deductions.

Universal life was marketed as the unbundling of whole life insurance. Insurance salespeople led consumers to believe that whole life was an overly expensive insurance policy.

Companies like A.L. Williams also attacked the insurance industry with their concept of buy term and invest the difference. Williams used a concept of a form of multi-level marketing, which amassed the largest part-time sales force in America. He would recruit people to sell insurance to three of their friends, who in turn sold to three of their friends, and so on. The justice department eventually arrested Art Williams for racketeering, and A.L. Williams Co. became Primerica. People have lost millions of dollars to these replacement artists, and insurance companies have lost control of the agents. This has led to many class action lawsuits. Meanwhile, the consumer remained uninformed, misinformed and in the dark as to what happened to their policies. Many people have not only lost their money, but many have also lost or will lose their insurance.

Universal life insurance is a flexible-premium, current-assumption, adjustable-death-benefit policy. Similar to traditional polices, universal life pays a death benefit and accumulates cash value. Unlike traditional products, universal life completely separates the protection element from the accumulation element of the policy.

Universal life is a combination of annual term insurance and a savings element. The amount of cash value will usually determine how long the policy will last or stay in force. As you get older, the term insurance cost goes up and the premium is withdrawn from the cash value. If the cash value is not sufficient to pay the term cost, your policy may terminate unless you pay in additional premiums. There are many variations of this product, and a thorough understanding of these provisions and how the interest is credited are critical for the proper results to happen. (Review **Illustrations #3** on pages 48 and 49, **#4A** and **B** on pages 50 to 53, **#5A** and **B** on pages 54 to 57, for further information). This type of insurance does not usually have nonforfeiture values. Nonforfeiture values are the guarantees usually found in whole life insurance and give you the ability to pay up the policy and guarantee a benefit with no more payments (see Whole Life term in **Appendix A**)

In May 2003, I published an article titled, "Widows Die Destitute Because of Loss of Husbands' Life Insurance." It brings the problem of not having guarantees in your life insurance to the forefront. To read the article, go to **Exhibit #1** on pages 125 and 126. Insurance companies are approaching the problem of lost insurance because of underfunding by guaranteeing the death benefit if you continue to pay a stated amount of premium; you must catch it up, or the guarantee does not apply. This approach is like putting a Band-Aid on a severed hand. The problem is, most people's finances greatly diminish in older age. Therefore, this approach only benefits the upper income buyers that have sufficient assets or income and have the ability to keep paying. The other part of the problem is there is no cash value at this point that would be available to help offset costs if money gets tight. When there is no cash value, and you have to keep paying, most will not continue the payments. Most of these types of insurance do not increase in death benefit when you pay extra premiums. Term insurance policies would cost more than the death benefit would pay. This is prevented by the required corridor (difference between the cash value and the death benefit) on universal life insurance policies, which eventually causes the death benefit to increase as the cash value increases.

Example #1 is a type-A policy with level death benefit. **Example #2** is a type-B policy, in which the death benefit is equal to the cash value and the face amount.

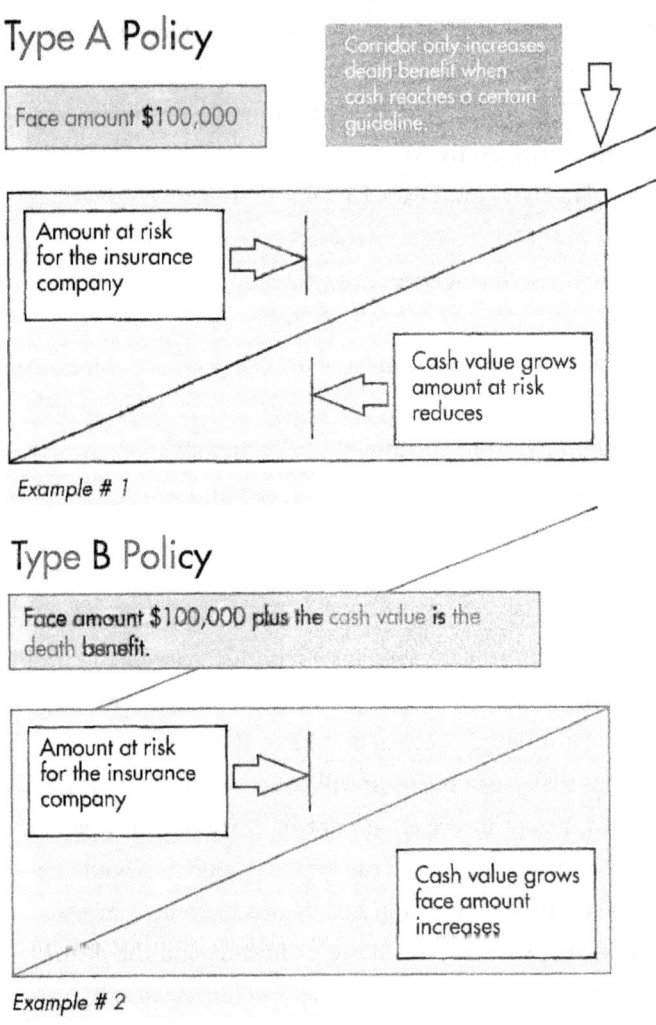

Example # 1

Example # 2

The positive aspect, if there is one with this insurance, is that the death benefits are paid income tax free, but this is usually the case with all life insurance. Interest rates in the 1980s were higher, and projections usually illustrated higher interest rates. When interest rates declined in the late 1980s and '90s, people found that their premiums had to be increased because the policies were underfunded. If the policies were underfunded and cash values declined, additional premium would be required to keep the policy in force.

Universal life consumers were not given proper disclosure or comparisons between universal life and guaranteed whole life. Universal life policies basically became a vehicle to replace, in many cases, high-quality cash value insurance with a nonforfeiture option.

When it all started:
The now defunct E.F. Hutton created universal life insurance in 1977 and took the market by storm. However, the great financial product the company created had little insurance benefit, and as I mentioned earlier, was mainly a savings account in an insurance policy wrapper. Fortunately for consumers who were blindly buying into this alleged be-all and end-all of replacement products, this type of insurance was eventually attacked by the competition and the government was forced to change the rules regarding how much cash value a policy could have in relation to the death benefit.

I believe the change brought on by the TAMRA Act greatly diminished the benefit of this type of policy. Sadly, the insurance companies had so much invested in the development of universal life, and realizing the profitability behind the concept, they still continue to sell this type of insurance, which is basically comprised of term insurance and a savings account. This could be the most profitable product the insurance industry sells.

How it Works
Basically, when you pay in a premium to the insurance company, they subtract expenses from the amount, and the balance goes into a savings fund (the bucket) where it earns interest. Each month, the

insurance company withdraws the appropriate amount to pay for the term insurance cost (mortality cost) of the policy and any other expenses, such as commissions or administration costs.

Some policies are securities-related, meaning the savings element can be invested in the financial markets. As long as there is money in the bucket, you have no problem with the policy. However, if the money runs out, as it will in many of the policies, you lose your money and the insurance. See appendix C for article explaining Index Universal Life.

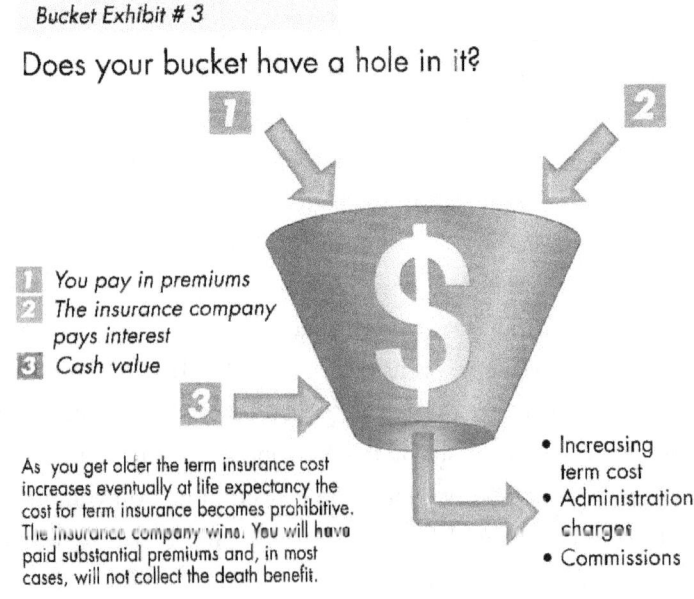

Bucket Exhibit # 3
Does your bucket have a hole in it?

1. You pay in premiums
2. The insurance company pays interest
3. Cash value

As you get older the term insurance cost increases eventually at life expectancy the cost for term insurance becomes prohibitive. The insurance company wins. You will have paid substantial premiums and, in most cases, will not collect the death benefit.

- Increasing term cost
- Administration charges
- Commissions

Bucket Exhibit # 4

Soon the cost is greater than your premium and eats up your cash value

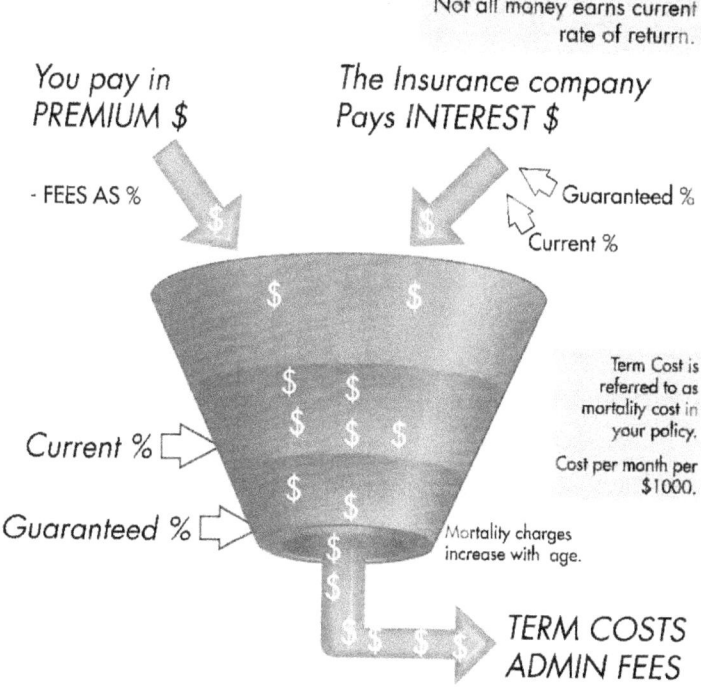

Ask yourself: Is my policy working? What is my purpose for the insurance? What is my goal? Inforce illustrations tell the story of how a policy will perform under current interest rates and insurance charges in the policy. These charges change constantly and require you to monitor the internal workings often. Will this policy work? That depends on many factors, such as how much you may have already paid, the interest rate credited, what is being credited now (current rate), and the current morality charges.

Can you fix your policy and make it work? Yes. Policies can be made to work in most cases by adjusting the level of premium being paid. However, sometimes premium payments are too far behind, and catching up would require some premiums than you're able or willing to pay. (See Life Insurance Goal Planning Worksheet on pages 127, 128 and 129).

CHAPTER FOUR

TERM LIFE INSURANCE

Term insurance is life insurance protection that expires after a specified term without any residual value if the insured survives the stated period. The protection period may be as short as thirty days (as in temporary insurance agreements) or as long as thirty years or more. (See sample illustrations on pages 73, 74 and 75). Term insurance may be decreasing, as in certain types of mortgage protection, or have a level benefit for the period. It may have a level premium or an increasing premium, often called Annual Renewable Term. This may be slated on the front cover or the first or second page of your policy. There are in essence dozens of variations of term insurance: one-year renewable, five-year renewable, ten-year renewable, etc. Some have increasing premiums and some have five, ten, twenty, and thirty-year periods of level premium. Term insurance may be the most expensive life insurance you could buy. Why? Because less than 1 percent is ever paid in a death claim, says a Penn State study completed in 1993. You pay all the premiums, and then when it does get more expensive you cancel the coverage by justifying you no longer need it. Imagine if life insurance had no economic cost to your lifestyle, and you could spend it on yourself before you die. The rate of return on your money could reach an average of 12 to 15 percent. In addition to the complexity are all the different riders that can be added. The most important one, in my opinion, is the Disability Waiver of Premium. This rider could guarantee the future success of your entire financial plan, or it could spell total defeat and failure. These riders are different and should be examined to see if there is a probability of receiving the benefit.

CHAPTER FIVE

LEVEL PREMIUM TERM LIFE INSURANCE POLICY

Many financial writers have advised the public for decades about the virtues of term life insurance. Their basic assumption is that term life insurance is low cost. Let's see if this is always true.

Term life insurance is generally promoted as a low-cost solution for those wanting to purchase life insurance. Many say buy term and invest the difference. But they never tell the buyer the real cost.

If I were 35 again, I could purchase a 20 years term life insurance policy with a guaranteed level premium of $590 per year. That would purchase $500,000 of coverage from a typical life insurance company.

Let's see if the premiums are really low cost. My premium of $590 for 20 years would total $11,800. This appears to be inexpensive. However, my family could lose over $700,000 if I don't die soon.

Let me explain. If I had decided to invest the $590 per years in a Roth IRA for the same 20 years, earning 8 percent, I could have as much as $29,160 at age 55. When I cancel the term life insurance policy at age 55, the premiums are not recovered, nor is any of the interest I could have earned.

Now, if I live to age 85, the $29,160 could have grown to $293,427. I didn't realize when I cancelled the policy that my family would most likely incur other expenses and opportunity Cost. The ultimate death benefit could have paid and prevented. Many times when I work with people at age forty-five, the real challenge is getting them to see things as a 55 or 65-year-old. Making decisions about the future is hard if we have no perception of what it will be like.

In this hypothetical example, the term policy could have cost me and my family approximately $793,427. The next illustration is a small term policy. Even a small policy can cost you hundreds of thousands in cost and lost interest. You will see if you look at **illustration #7C** on page 75, the total cost of the insurance would exceed eight times the face amount.

Illustrations 7A, 7B, and 7C show an example of a Term illustration for a 35 year old male for $500,000 of a 20 year level premium term life insurance policy.

LIFE INSURANCE: WILL IT PAY WHEN I DIE?

Selec Term 20
Annual Renewable Term Insurance to Age 98

Illustration 7A

Designed For: **Tom Young** / Male/ Age 35 / Non-Tobacco

Policy values are based on the policy, riders and benefits shown on Page 8. All premiums are assumed to be paid out-of-pocket. No loans or partial surrenders are taken from policy.

Initial Specified Amount = $500,000.00
Total Initial Annual Premium = $590.00
Premium Mode = Annual

Guaranteed Values

End of Year	Age	Annualized Contract Premium	Death Benefit
1	36	590	500,000
2	37	590	500,000
3	38	590	500,000
4	39	590	500,000
5	40	590	500,000
6	41	590	500,000
7	42	590	500,000
8	43	590	500,000
9	44	590	500,000
10	45	590	500,000
11	46	590	500,000
12	47	590	500,000
13	48	590	500,000
14	49	590	500,000
15	50	590	500,000
16	51	590	500,000
17	52	590	500,000
18	53	590	500,000
19	54	590	500,000
20	55	590	500,000
21	56	6,545	500,000
22	57	7,190	500,000
23	58	7,885	500,000
24	59	8,675	500,000
25	60	9,550	500,000
26	61	10,525	500,000
27	62	11,635	500,000
28	63	12,905	500,000
29	64	14,335	500,000
30	65	15,920	500,000
31	66	17,620	500,000
32	67	19,465	500,000
33	68	21,445	500,000
34	69	23,605	500,000
35	70	26,045	500,000

Selec Term 20
Annual Renewable Term Insurance to Age 98

Illustration 7B

Designed For: **Tom Young** / Male / Age 35 / Non-Tobacco

Policy values are based on the policy, riders and benefits shown on Page 8. All premiums are assumed to be paid out-of-pocket. No loans or partial surrenders are taken from policy.

Initial Specified Amount = $500,000.00
Total Initial Annual Premium = $590.00
Premium Mode = Annual

End of Year	Age	Guaranteed Values	
		Annualized Contract Premium	Death Benefit
36	71	28,750	500,000
37	72	31,990	500,000
38	73	35,650	500,000
39	74	39,760	500,000
40	75	44,170	500,000
41	76	48,865	500,000
42	77	53,800	500,000
43	78	58,925	500,000
44	79	64,360	500,000
45	80	70,325	500,000
46	81	76,960	500,000
47	82	84,460	500,000
48	83	92,915	500,000
49	84	102,155	500,000
50	85	111,970	500,000
51	86	122,170	500,000
52	87	132,665	500,000
53	88	143,240	500,000
54	89	154,040	500,000
55	90	165,215	500,000
56	91	176,950	500,000
57	92	189,635	500,000
58	93	203,795	500,000
59	94	221,810	500,000
60	95	247,540	500,000
61	96	288,485	500,000
62	97	360,220	500,000
63	98	493,555	500,000

	Guaranteed		Assumed	
	10 Year	20 Year	10 Year	20 Year
Surrender Cost Index:	1.18	1.18	1.18	1.18
Net Payment Index:	1.18	1.18	1.18	1.18

LIFE INSURANCE: WILL IT PAY WHEN I DIE?

Illustration 7C

Selec Term 20

MTL Insurance Company

Annual Renewable Term Insurance to Age 98
Supplemental Illustration

Designed For: **Tom Young** / Male / Age 35 / Non-Tobacco

Initial Specified Amount = $500,000.00
Total Initial Annual Premium = $590.00
Premium Mode = Annual

Summary Illustration

Age / Year	Annual Net Outlay	Cumulative Net Outlay	Death Benefit
1 / 36	$ 590.00	$ 590.00	500,000
5 / 40	$ 590.00	$ 2,959.00	500,000
10 / 45	$ 590.00	$ 5,900.00	500,000
15 / 50	$ 590.00	$ 8,850.00	500,000
20 / 55	$ 590.00	$ 11,800.00	500,000
30 / 65	$ 15,920.00	$ 116,965.00	500,000
63 / 98	$ 493,555.00	$ 4,069,520.00	500,000

CHAPTER SIX

VARIABLE LIFE INSURANCE

Variable life insurance is similar to universal life insurance in that it is made up of a term insurance element and a savings element. The savings element is typically invested into accounts called side funds, which are similar to mutual funds. Many insurance companies hire the same management that manages our mutual funds. This brings the risk of loss. This not only introduces the risk of interest variables to the account, it also adds investment risk. Life insurance is meant to be a protection vehicle, not an investment shelter.

The government is currently looking into the variable products that are offered and are questioning the tax-deferred status of these types of products. I believe governmental restrictions will eventually be imposed to stop the proliferation of this type of insurance, just as they were with the first types of universal life insurance products that looked and worked like tax-deferred savings accounts.

Basically, the policy includes an account, called savings or side fund, and the cost of insurance is deducted from that account. If you run out of money, the contract will potentially lapse. Then you lose your coverage and the money you have paid in.

CHAPTER SEVEN

WHOLE LIFE INSURANCE

According to industry sources, forty-one percent of adults in the United States have no life insurance, and thirty-three percent of U.S. families say they don't have enough life insurance to protect their loved ones if a primary wage earner in the family were to die.

When I meet with clients, and we "dream in color" about their hopes and aspirations and what they want to see happen, the discussion will often lead to the need for life insurance. I'm always asked, "Tom, what is the best policy I can buy?" My response is always that I believe the "best" life insurance policy to have is the one that's in force on the day you die. The life insurance industry has done an amazing job creating an array of products: term, universal, variable, indexed universal, and whole life. While every client and situation are different, I am convinced that for long-term financial peace of mind, a participating (dividend-eligible) whole life offers a flexible foundation with guarantees and living benefits that offer you certainty in an uncertain world. An industry study reported that buyers prefer whole life insurance because "…it's straight forward and offers premium and cash value guarantees, along with lifetime coverage."

The central advantages of a participating whole life insurance policy revolves around the ironclad contractual guarantees: a guaranteed death benefit, which is typically income-tax-free to beneficiaries; a guaranteed, level premium that will never increase for the life of the contract as long as you continue to pay premiums; guaranteed cash values that accumulate on a tax-deferred basis and will never decline because of changes in the financial markets; and the guaranteed non-forfeiture provisions that allow you long-term exit strategies.

I've mentioned that my preference is for whole life policies that are "participating." What this means is they are offered by a mutual life insurance company where the policyowners (that's you!) share in the ownership of the company. In a stock company, the shareholders are the "owners," and typically decisions made by management are based on short-term goals. Mutual companies, however, can make decisions based on more long-term objectives. Dividends, by law, are not guaranteed. However, most mutual companies pass on a portion of their earnings once a year to policyowners by distributing dividends. This is why the financial strength, history, and management of the company you choose is very important. Once declared, the dividends are now guaranteed. Once they've been declared and are in your policy, they are yours. This is where the flexibility and living benefits that dividends offer can really enhance your financial world. Whole life policies offer contractual options for dividends, and these options can be changed through the years as your needs change. They can be sent to you in cash, they can reduce the premium, they can purchase more insurance ("paid up additions"), and they can accumulate at interest.

Whole life is life insurance offering protection for the whole of life with proceeds payable at death. Premiums may be paid under a continuous premium arrangement or on a limited payment basis for virtually any desired period of years (e.g., one, ten, twenty, thirty, or to ages sixty or sixty-five).

This type of insurance includes ownership provisions called non-forfeiture provisions. Whole life insurance has guarantees that other types of insurance do not. The premium is guaranteed, the cash value is guaranteed, and the death benefit is guaranteed. These guarantees can sometimes provide leverage for other events in life. See **illustration #8A** and **8B** on pages 82-83 and 84-85.

So, whole life is just what it says: life insurance for the whole life, guaranteed. Many forms of life insurance being sold today are marked as permanent with guarantees. However, other types of life insurance, especially universal life, do not carry the same guarantees as whole life.

Many policies have been sold on the common belief that the benefits of life insurance can't be realized until death. It was never explained that whole life insurance has living values associated with the policy.

For example, if you had a credit card with an ongoing balance that was casting you eighteen percent interest, you could borrow from the life insurance company, using your life insurance as collateral. The interest cost would be usually between five and seven percent. At the same time, your policy would continue to receive dividends and increase in cash value (participating policy). The internal rate of return in your policy would average between three and six percent over your lifetime. The cost of borrowing would be a net cost of one to three percent. Hence, if you're paying 18 percent to the credit card on your $2,000 average balance, your interest cost would be $2,000 x 18 percent = $360, versus $2,000 x 2 percent = $40, giving you an average cost recovery of $320. If you did this every year for 30 years, earning an average of 6 percent net of taxes, you would have $26,816.54 at 65 and at age 85 the amount saved would be $180,837.08.

This is only one small disciplined way to recover wealth. Anyone who earns above poverty-level income and practices discipline over his or her lifetime can recover a minimum of $1 million (See Chapter 8: Opportunity Cost of Money).

Level Premium Whole Life Insurance Paid Up at

Designed For: **Tom Young** / Male/ Age 45 / Non-Tobacco

Policy values are based on the policy, riders and benefits shown in the Narrative Summary. All premiums are assumed to be paid out-of-pocket. No loans or partial surrenders are taken from policy.

End of Year	Age	Annualized Contract Premium	Guaranteed Values	
			Cash Surrender Value	Death Benefit
1	46	2,060	0	100,000
2	47	2,060	808	100,000
3	48	2,060	2,752	100,000
4	49	2,060	4,754	100,000
5	50	2,060	6,812	100,000
6	51	2,060	8,608	100,000
7	52	2,060	10,443	100,000
8	53	2,060	12,314	100,000
9	54	2,060	14,218	100,000
10	55	2,060	16,150	100,000
11	56	2,060	18,110	100,000
12	57	2,060	20,097	100,000
13	58	2,060	22,119	100,000
14	59	2,060	24,158	100,000
15	60	2,060	26,735	100,000
16	61	2,060	28,333	100,000
17	62	2,060	30,454	100,000
18	63	2,060	32,585	100,000
19	64	2,060	34,744	100,000
20	65	2,060	36,896	100,000
21	66	1,938	39,049	100,000
22	67	1,938	41,102	100,000
23	68	1,938	43,358	100,000
24	69	1,938	45,517	100,000
25	70	1,938	47,679	100,000
26	71	1,938	49,694	100,000
27	72	1,938	51,912	100,000
28	73	1,938	54,105	100,000
29	74	1,938	56,186	100,000
30	75	1,938	58,217	100,000
31	76	1,938	60,196	100,000
32	77	1,938	62,127	100,000
33	78	1,938	64,020	100,000
34	79	1,938	65,888	100,000
35	80	1,938	67,742	100,000

LIFE INSURANCE: WILL IT PAY WHEN I DIE?

Age 90

Basic Illustration

Illustration 8A

Initial Specified Amount = $100,000.00
Total Initial Annual Premium = $2,060.00
Premium Mode = Annual
Dividend Option = Paid Up Additions

Total Values Including Non-Guaranteed Assumptions*

Annual Dividend	Cash Surrender Value	Death Benefit
0	0	100,000
40	848	100,121
55	2,848	100,280
72	4,926	100,484
100	7,089	100,756
145	9,039	101,138
209	11,098	101,674
281	13,271	102,371
353	15,559	103,219
431	17,965	104,222
497	20,478	105,344
554	23,091	106,558
611	25,808	107,857
669	28,630	109,240
746	31,581	110,738
832	34,666	112,361
933	37,900	114,134
1,042	41,286	116,060
1,165	44,833	118,156
1,298	48,546	120,432
1,441	52,437	122,896
1,585	56,508	125,540
1,730	60,765	128,359
1,870	65,207	131,335
2,028	69,853	134,489
2,217	74,729	137,862
2,425	79,846	141,471
2,659	85,215	145,348
2,915	90,842	149,513
3,182	96,725	153,973
3,429	102,841	158,693
3,690	109,210	163,684
3,941	115,833	168,927
4,185	122,723	174,406
4,436	129,900	180,124

Level Premium Whole Life Insurance Paid Up at

| | | | Guaranteed Values | |
End of Year	Age	Annualized Contract Premium	Cash Surrender Value	Death Benefit
36	81	1,938	69,584	100,000
37	82	1,938	71,415	100,000
38	83	1,938	73,229	100,000
39	84	1,938	75,029	100,000
40	85	1,938	76,813	100,000
41	86	1,938	79,623	100,000
42	87	1,938	80,504	100,000
43	88	1,938	82,520	100,000
44	89	1,938	84,782	100,000
45	90	1,938	87,437	100,000
46	91	0	88,270	100,000
47	92	0	89,148	100,000
48	93	0	90,078	100,000
49	94	0	91,102	100,000
50	95	0	92,250	100,000
51	96	0	93,525	100,000
52	97	0	94,022	100,000
53	98	0	96,400	100,000
54	99	0	97,816	100,000
55	100	0	100,000	100,000

	Guaranteed	
	10 Year	20 Year
Surrender Cost Index:	7.15	8.75
Net Payment Index:	19.38	19.38

LIFE INSURANCE: WILL IT PAY WHEN I DIE?

Age 90

Illustration 8B

Total Values Including Non-Guaranteed Assumptions*

Annual Dividend	Cash Surrender Value	Death Benefit
4,709	137,389	186,104
5,003	145,206	192,366
5,332	153,372	198,949
5,695	161,908	205,889
6,057	170,814	213,182
6,415	180,113	220,819
6,762	189,842	228,783
7,081	200,054	237,039
7,366	210,834	245,544
7,616	222,313	254,255
7,672	232,118	262,946
7,902	242,312	271,810
7,824	252,665	280,496
7,675	263,215	288,921
7,457	273,983	297,005
7,459	285,240	304,980
7,565	297,064	312,949
7,736	309,398	320,975
7,832	321,797	328,982
5,438	334,420	334,420

Assumed

10 Year	20 Year
5.28	4.02
17.51	14.65

* These values are based on the Current Interest Rate of 4.00% and the Current Monthly Deductions.

HOW TO READ THE ANNUAL STATEMENT

The annual statement is the starting point for evaluating the performance of your insurance policy. As previously mentioned, along with your annual statement, you should request an inforce illustration, which should be ordered in a couple formats.

First, ask for a projection using the current premium you are actually paying—not the one scheduled on the face page of the policy—the one you actually intend to pay. This is the projection policy and the current morality costs associated with your policy. This projection should run to at least age ninety.

Second, request an illustration on how much premium would be required to be paid to have the policy endow at age one hundred, which means the face amount of the policy would equal the case value at age one hundred. This would give you the safest position to be sure, under most policies, that your policy would last until age one hundred. The most conservative position would be to endow the policy at age one hundred using the guaranteed interest rates and values.

I will provide you with a written explanation of your illustrations and annual statement if you send them to 1st Consultants, Inc. You will receive these illustrations with your check for $39.95 payable to Thomas W. Young, 1413 Third Street Beaver, PA 15009.

Let's look at the statements I've included here. This first illustration is a case that I recently worked on. The names and circumstances have been changed to protect the privacy of my client.

Mr. Kelley, a successful business owner, purchased a policy at age fifty-one. The original illustration shows substantial gains in cash value all through the years of the projected period of time. The interest rates were much higher than today. The projection included some rollover cash values from other insurance policies that were cancelled. The projection included a premium of $254 per month.

About four or five years into the plan, Mr. Kelley became disabled and filed for the benefits under waiver of premium. This was a big benefit and the same coverage in a whole life plan would have paid the premium and been guaranteed by the insurance for Mr. Kelley. However, under universal life, the waiver of premium was for a stated amount—the amount Mr. Kelley was paying.

It looked good in the beginning. However, Mr. Kelley had recently had severe medical problems and was concerned about losing the policy and the benefit. The policy that was to have lots of cash was now in jeopardy of lapsing for lack of money. In fact, the policy could have ended in February 2004, even though over $100,000 have been paid in premiums. See **illustrations #9A** and **#9B** on pages 90, 91 and 92.

More than twenty-seven thousand dollars had been paid as the waiver premium benefit. An additional ninety-six thousand dollars was paid into the policy, and it still had run out of cash. Mr. Kelley was now sixty-eight years old, and the estate planning he had done would be forfeited without the policy death benefit.

The good side of this is that Mr. Kelley was able to pay the now-required premium of over $18,000 per year. Mr. Kelley was lucky, but how many of you could have paid ten times your current premium to keep the insurance?

This is the same problem I wrote about in the article. A person would retire, take the single option on his pension, and buy a large life insurance policy to protect his spouse, should he die prematurely. Many agents have done a bad thing in replacing a guaranteed benefit with a non-guaranteed policy.

Illustration #9A shows:
The third column is the planned premiums.

The fourth and fifth columns are projected using ten percent interest for the cash value and death benefit.

The sixth and seventh columns assume the middle-of-the-road approach of 8.5 percent for both the cash value and death benefit.

The eighth and ninth columns are based on guaranteed maximum cost of insurance and crediting with the minimum amount of interest at 4.5 percent. These columns are the most interesting. Follow the difference between the cast value at 10 percent and the cash value at 4.5 percent at age 71. Life insurance for the long term should always be permanent guaranteed participation whole life insurance. This type of insurance would have nonforfeiture values and would permit the contract to be paid up.

Even at the beginning of the projection, a prudent person would have to look at long-term averages of fixed interest rates and find the average under 4.5 percent. Expecting the market to sustain high interest rates over a long term is pie in the sky. The historical average of the stock market is only 6 to 8 percent, if you exclude the anomaly of the 1990s.

LIFE INSURANCE: WILL IT PAY WHEN I DIE?

UNIVERSAL LIFE
FLEXIBLE PREMIUM ADJUSTABLE LIFE INSURANCE

Illustration 9A

Prepared For: Mr. Kelley
Prepared By:

Initial Stated Amount: $500,000
Level Death Benefit: Ages 51-95

CURRENT COST OF INSURANCE
Current Interest of 10.000%
—End of Year—

Age	Year	Planned Premium Outlay For Year (a)	Cash Value	Death Benefit
52	1	67,100	71,053	500,000
53	2	33,100	110,364	500,000
54	3	3,100	122,308	500,000
55	4	3,100	135,500	500,000
56	5	48,100	197,350	500,000
57	6	3,100	218,448	500,000
58	7	3,100	241,759	500,000
59	8	3,100	267,515	500,000
60	9	3,100	295,977	500,000
61	10	3,100	327,697	500,000
62	11	3,100	362,304	500,000
63	12	3,100	400,526	504,663
64	13	3,100	442,472	548,665
65	14	21,900-	463,339	565,273
66	15	25,000-	482,833	579,400
71	20	25,000-	610,326	701,875
76	25	25,000-	814,760	855,498
81	30	25,000-	1,140,964	1,198,012
82	31	25,000-	1,225,228	1,289,489
83	32	25,000-	1,317,113	1,382,969
84	33	25,000-	1,417,248	1,488,111

THOMAS W. YOUNG

Illustration 9A

Classification: Nonsmoker
Male - Age 51

CURRENT COST OF INSURANCE Assumed Interest of 8.500% —End of Year—		Guaranteed Cost of Insurance and Guaranteed Interest of 4.500% —End of Year—	
Cash Value	Death Benefit	Cash Value	Death Benefit
70,066	500,000	67,434	500,000
107,764	500,000	99,954	500,000
117,785	500,000	103,869	500,000
128,700	500,000	107,635	500,000
187,221	500,000	156,367	500,000
204,401	500,000	163,317	500,000
223,118	500,000	168,228	500,000
243,512	500,000	174,089	500,000
265,735	500,000	179,880	500,000
290,219	500,000	185,834	500,000
316,329	500,000	191,692	500,000
344,665	500,000	197,404	500,000
375,344	500,000	202,912	500,000
383,772	475,000	183,161	475,000
389,829	472,795	158,801	450,000
427,184	491,262	5,074	325,000
484,251	508,464	0	0
570,023	598,524	0	0
591,071	620,625	0	0
613,607	644,287	0	0
637,718	669,604	0	0

LIFE INSURANCE: WILL IT PAY WHEN I DIE?

Illustration 9B

ANNUAL REPORT

Statement Date: 10/10/2002
Policy Number:
Policy Date: 9/28/1986
Planned Maturity: 9/28/2030

Statement Period
From: 9/28/2001
To: 9/28/2002

SUMMARY OF COVERAGE

Insured -

	As of 09/28/2001	As of 09/28/2002
Primary Insured Death Benefit (Assuming no loan)	$500,000.00	$500,000.00
Primary Insured Death Benefit (With affect of loan)	$500,000.00	$500,000.00
Policy Value	$18,004.63	$12,143.01
Surrender Charge	$0.00	$0.00
Outstanding Loan	$0.00	$0.00
Surrender Value	$18,004.63	$12,143.01

The Guaranteed Interest Rate is 4.50%
The Current Interest Rate as of 10/28/2002 is 5.85%
The Death Benefit Option is Level.

Since the Annual Report you received from us on your last policy anniversary, your interest rate for some month(s) decreased. Please see Transaction Details on reverse side.

CONTINUATION OF INSURANCE

Coverage will terminate assuming:	Guaranteed Interest and Mortality Charge	Current Interest and Mortality Charge
No more premiums are paid	7/28/2003	10/28/2003
Planned premiums* are continued	9/28/2003	2/28/2004

Set to expire on

THOMAS W. YOUNG

Illustration 9B

CONTINUATION OF INSURANCE

These projections assume that you are planning to pay premiums continuously during the lifetime of the insured. If you plan to pay otherwise, please contact the Home Office for information concerning the continuation of your coverage.

> IMPORTANT: BASED ON CURRENT INTEREST AND MORTALITY ASSUMPTIONS, THIS POLICY WILL TERMINATE ON 02/28/2004. PLEASE CONTACT US FOR ADDITIONAL INFORMATION.

Also, your policy will terminate in the next year using guaranteed interest and mortality charge. If no more premiums are paid. The amount which must be paid to keep the policy in force until the next anniversary under these assumptions is $2,673.47.

The planned premium for this policy is $253.87 per month. If premiums are paid as scheduled and we continue to pay interest at the current rate, your policy value as of 09/28/2003 will be $4,456.04. This projected value is not guaranteed.

> IMPORTANT POLICY OWNER NOTICE: You should consider requesting more detailed information about your policy to understand how it may perform in the future. You should not consider replacement of your policy or make changes in your coverage without requesting a current illustration. You may annually request, without charge, such an illustration by contacting your agent, calling 1-800-xxx-xxxx, or writing to us. If you do not receive a current illustration of your policy within 30 days from your request, you should contact your state insurance department.

THE ANNUAL STATEMENT

This statement is the basic information you need to start to understand and determine the health of your universal life insurance policy.

Illustration 10

Summary of Transactions for Year Ending 12/26/2002

POLICY TRANSACTIONS

Effective Date	Transaction Type	⬇1 Amount	⬇2 Expense Charges	⬇3 Premium for Riders	⬇4 Net Amount
12/27/2001	PREM	$91.04	$8.93	$8.93	$73.18
12/27/2001 1/27/2002	PREM	$91.04	$8.93	$8.93	$73.18
1/27/2002 2/27/2002	PREM	$91.04	$8.93	$8.93	$73.18
2/27/2002 3/27/2002	PREM	$91.04	$8.93	$8.93	$73.18
3/27/2002 4/27/2002	PREM	$91.04	$8.93	$8.93	$73.18
4/27/2002 5/27/2002	PREM	$91.04	$8.93	$8.93	$73.18
5/27/2002 6/27/2002	PREM	$91.04	$8.93	$8.93	$73.18
6/27/2002 7/27/2002	PREM	$91.04	$8.93	$8.93	$73.18
7/27/2002 8/27/2002	PREM	$91.04	$8.93	$8.93	$73.18
8/27/2002 9/27/2002	PREM	$91.04	$8.93	$8.93	$73.18
9/27/2002 10/27/2002	PREM	$91.04	$8.93	$8.93	$73.18
10/27/2002 11/27/2002	PREM	$91.04	$8.93	$8.93	$73.18
11/27/2002 TOTAL			$107.16	$107.16	$878.16

* If N/A is shown, it means that item is not applicable to your policy.

MONTHLY DEDUCTIONS		POLICY VALUES		
⬇5	⬇6	⬇7	⬇8	⬇9
		INTERESTED CREDITED		
Insurance Costs Insured	Admin.* Charge	Unloaned Amount 4.50%	Loaned Amount 6.00%	Policy Account
$38.11	N/A	$38.11	$0.00	$18,168.64
$37.99	N/A	$37.99	$0.00	$18,272.01
$37.86	N/A	$37.86	$0.00	$18,369.25
$37.75	N/A	$37.75	$0.00	$18,473.61
$37.62	N/A	$37.62	$0.00	$18,576.25
$37.50	N/A	$37.50	$0.00	$18,681.64
$37.37	N/A	$37.37	$0.00	$18,785.29
$37.25	N/A	$37.25	$0.00	$18,891.71
$37.12	N/A	$37.12	$0.00	$18,998.66
$36.99	N/A	$36.99	$0.00	$19,103.84
$36.87	N/A	$36.87	$0.00	$19,211.84
$36.74	N/A	$36.74	$0.00	$19,318.04
$449.17	N/A	$449.17	$0.00	

LIFE INSURANCE: WILL IT PAY WHEN I DIE?

Illustration 10 *continued*

Table of Interest Rates

	12/27/01 to 12/26/02	12/27/02 to 12/26/03
Policy Account		
Rate Credited on Unloaned Amounts *	4.50 %	4.25 %
Rate Credited on Loaned Amounts *	6.00 %	6.00 %
Policy Loans		
Rate Charged on Policy Loans *	8.00 %	8.00 %

* These are effective annual interest rates.

> Notice: There has been a decrease in the nonguaranteed interest rate for your policy. You should consider requesting an in force illustration of policy values based on your policy's status.

Projected Values as of 12/26/2003
Based on the Nonguaranteed Interest Rate of 4.25%

Face Amount	$50,000	Policy Account	$20,534.76
Death Benefit	$91.04	Cash Value	$20,534.76

Termination Dates
Your policy will terminate on or about the following date:

Guaranteed Basis Assuming	4.00%	12/26/2027
Nonguaranteed Basis Assuming	4.25%	LIFE

The first column is the amount of premiums paid monthly during the year. The second column is expense charges, including any commissions or fees charged. The third column is premiums for any riders, such as a spouse rider or children's rider. Next, we have the net amount column and then the insurance charges for the death benefit. The administration or premium charges column is next. Then we see the interest credited to the cash value with different rates for borrowed and non-borrowed funds. Finally, the last column is the cash value by the month. This column should tell you a lot about your policy. Look at the values in the first month compared to the cash value in the last month. Has the policy increased in value, stayed the same, or has the value declined? The net increase is where we start. The net increase is the gross premium paid, less any expenses, commissions, and insurance charges.

Look in the policy for the page marked "monthly morality charges per thousand." Find the maximum rate the insurance company could charge. Multiply the net amount of insurance in thousands by the monthly rate, and then multiply that by twelve months. This amount is the maximum insurance charge the insurance company could charge you. The question is, how much cash value do you need to be able to pay the insurance charges? Take the amount and divide by the interest rate being credited. The table of guaranteed maximum insurance rates are on page 100.

See page 100. The factor is 14.325 per thousand. This time let's say 100,000 less 13,000 of cash value. That's 87.000 times 14.325, and the answer is $1,246.28 per month. Now multiply by 12 months for a total of $14,955.30 yearly morality charge. You would need $299,106 of capital earning 5 percent interest to generate the cash flow to cover the insurance costs at age 85 ($13,168.2 divided by 5 percent interest).

The annual statement marked **Illustration #10** on pages 94, 95, 96 and 97 is a well-funded healthy policy. The cash value is equal to

40 percent of the death benefit, and if you read the section called termination dates, you'll find that under the guarantee of 4 percent, the policy will work until 2027. However, at the current rate of 4.25 percent and current morality charges, the policy will be in force for life.

This further illustrates that small differences in interest rates can have huge effects on the future viability of the policy.

If we look at Mr. Kelley's annual report (**Illustration #9B**) on page 92, we find it will expire in February 2004 because it will run out of cash. This is an example of underfunding of the policy. when the policy has run out of money and morality costs are beyond the scope of comprehension. Look at the original illustration to see how much cash was projected from the beginning. It didn't even come close. The company should have at least informed the client as to the changes in projected value.

The companies expect you, the consumer, to understand and manage these types of accounts. If many of the agents don't know the answers themselves, how in the world can they expect the consumer to figure this out?

Illustration 11

Table of Guaranteed Maximum Rates For Each $1000 of Term Insurance
(Sometimes referred to as Mortality Charges.)

AGE	MONTHLY RATE* MALE	MONTHLY RATE* FEMALE	AGE	MONTHLY RATE* MALE	MONTHLY RATE* FEMALE
27	.143	.103	75	5.785	3.445
28	.142	.107	76	6.359	3.869
29	.143	.110	77	6.958	4.325
30	.146	.114	78	7.585	4.819
31	.150	.118	79	8.262	5.370
32	.156	.123	80	9.012	6.000
33	.163	.128	81	9.958	6.729
34	.171	.134	82	10.822	7.579
35	.181	.142	83	11.902	8.549
36	.194	.152	84	13.077	9.626
37	.208	.163	85	14.325	10.811
38	.224	.178	86	15.626	12.091
39	.242	.194	87	16.976	13.469
40	.263	.211	88	18.375	14.952
41	.285	.229	89	19.834	16.556
42	.310	.249	90	21.379	18.306

PART 2

CHAPTER EIGHT

OPPORTUNITY COST OF MONEY

Let's start with the principal of opportunity cost, which implies that the value or cost of a resource used in one particular application is determined by what its use in the best alternative gives up. The basis for understanding this concept is recognizing that every act of choice also involves an act of sacrifice.

Opportunity cost can be compared to taking off work to go to a football game. The game ticket costs ten dollars, but you could have worked and earned thirty dollars. Thus, the cost of going to the game is forty dollars. However, the game had a psychic benefit greater than the thirty dollars lost from work.

Consider a few more examples. Someone with a high income would be more likely to hire someone to cut grass than someone with a low income would, and low-income people would travel long distance by car or bus.

High-income professionals may earn two hundred or three hundred dollars an hour. They would pay someone twenty dollars an hour to cut their grass or to do some other job. It is expensive for a professional to spend time riding on a bus, writing letters, or working around the house doing odd jobs. Thus, the relevant cost for selecting an optimal choice alternative is not only the cash expenditure, but also the opportunity cost involved by foregoing something else.

You are inundated with marketing noise about products and services. The advertising world makes their fortune by getting you to believe their product or service will solve all your problems or make your dreams come true. The products and services we use in our financial lives are seldom in our best interest. To purchase a product and not truly understand what to do or how to maximize the economic results, would leave you just spending money to be average—just doing what everyone else is doing. Do you remember the statistic that says one out of one hundred gets rich? Well, continuing to do what everyone else is doing assures you a place in the ninety-nine out of one hundred who don't get rich.

To get from where you are to some perceived financial level of success in the future, you will need to learn to manage the leaks of your life. Money leaks out in many ways. Think of it like a bucket with holes in it. Most people work their whole lives trying to make more and more money, not realizing there is an economic limit based on education, experience, and most importantly, how you think. You don't focus on fixing the holes in the bucket. The key to becoming wealthy has little to do with how much you make; it has more to do with how you think.

The decisions you make are always at the expense of something else. Time or money directed toward something or someplace takes away from something or someplace else. Opportunity costs are created by many of these decisions and go unnoticed. We have not been trained to look for or even understand opportunity costs. Think of it as three different people starting their adult lives all with the same income, but each one ending up differently.

Robert Castiglione, of LEAP Systems, once said, "The how decisions you make set the stage for these differences in results, not the where decisions. We use a very broad spectrum of products and services in our lives. I believe the secret is more in the synergism of these products and services, not in the products themselves. By using this concept, it is possible that the sum of the parts equal more than the whole."

The first thing you need to dramatically improve your financial results is a system to enable you to accurately evaluate a products performance and measure its results in real economic terms.

Weigh the macroeconomic verses the microeconomic. The products must be valued together, not just by themselves, but also as part of a strategic master plan. A translator in a circuit board is not very exciting by itself, but put that transistor in NASA's hands and it can send a shuttle into space. The right financial plan can change your life, make your dreams seem within reach, and help you live a fulfilling life of success and happiness.

Evaluating products' values using the theories we are taught by the financial institutions flaws our perception because we only compare one product with another. The true evaluation comes when we understand that all products coordinate with others in our synergistic macroeconomic lives.

On the surface, a practice like buying term insurance and investing the difference makes so much sense. However, the truth is that term insurance should be used for short-term solutions to human life value goals until you can create enough wealth and cash flow to purchase participating whole life insurance.

A Pennsylvania State University study showed that less than 1 percent of term insurance is ever paid in a death claim. Synergism helps us to find the multiplier effect of our financial lives.

In economics we learn about the velocity of money and the multiplier effect. This boils down to the Federal Reserve System in America. The banks and financial institutions use this system of checkable deposits to multiply their money on paper. You put a dollar in the bank, and they pay you some interest. They loan it out on paper several times and make money on each transaction. Check out a bank's financial statement and you will find they make as much as 30, 40, 50 percent, or more on the money.

We as individuals can't do what the banks do, but we can certainly use our dollars toward more than one purpose. Say items A and B each cost a dollar. Then you find out item C also costs a dollar, and it will do the jobs of both items A and B. That's a 100 percent rate of return.

We expect people to make correct decisions when they have accurate information. Unfortunately, the marketing noise I mentioned earlier is the only information most of us have at our disposal when trying to make informed decisions.

I have had successful clients move their accounts because of the influence of the marketing noise; the new product sounds more exciting than what we were doing previously. The one thing they forgot was the evaluation process of macroeconomics—looking at the sum of the parts to determine the effectiveness of the whole. They got all caught up in the exciting product and forgot the real return comes in how a product works with their other financial products. This centers on the theory of rational choice. The cost and benefit argument based on subjective measures sometimes gives us a clouded picture. These decisions cannot be evaluated in isolation.

"The macroeconomic model must include all the financial components of our lives. An engine would not perform to the optimum without all parts functioning properly," says Robert Castiglione. "Let's go to the true heart of a financial model: life insurance. That is, participating whole life insurance. The fuel pump sends its life-supporting energy to the engine. Similarly, the human body would not be healthy unless all the organs were functioning properly. The heart acts as the fuel pump, sending life-supporting blood to the body. In a financial plan, all your assets need to be working properly, and whole life acts as the heart of the financial model", says Castiglione.

Participating whole life is the most efficient macroeconomic wealth creation, enhancement, and human life value instrument available. Other so-called forms of permanent life insurance will not provide all the same benefits. Isn't it interesting that so many class action lawsuits have been filed against all the other products the insurance industry sells?

I've included an illustration of a basic participating whole life policy in pages 82 through 85. Let me start by explaining the product's three guarantees.

First, the premiums are guaranteed. No one can change them in any way at any time. this is important to understand because it means the real rate of cost becomes a declining cost due to inflation. You get an increasing benefit and a declining cost. A premium of one hundred dollars ten years ago is like fifty dollars today. The real cost actually reduces due to inflation.

Second, the cash value is guaranteed. That means you have a guaranteed future source of capital, and most importantly, it can become a reserve. The return can reach as much as twelve to fifteen percent when used to recover other costs in your life.

Third, the death benefit is guaranteed. This guarantee can be a powerful leverage tool as you get older. We all know we are going to die. Knowing you have a guaranteed death benefit gives you a powerful leverage tool. I'll explain more as we go along.

The fourth element, dividends paid by the insurance company, is not guaranteed but has always been there in some amount. What is a dividend? In an insurance policy, the dividend by a tax law is a return of premium and is therefore not taxable. However, it can become taxable if withdrawn from the policy in cash and if it exceeds the amount you've paid in premiums. Gee, it's beginning to sound like there is some profit available here. That's right. Over time the average participating whole life policy will have an internal rate of return of three to five percent. The dividend is derived from the profits of the insurance company. They're not guaranteed, but they have been paid every year, even during the depression.

The guarantee becomes important in your overall financial plan because you can use the death benefit as a powerful living benefit. There are hidden costs rarely disclosed to us that are associated with the compounding of money.

I'll discuss several concepts here. Remember that the real rate of return is not from one micro part of your plan but in the harmony the different parts perform together.

CHAPTER NINE

PENSION MAXIMIZATION

Pension maximization has been a very popular sales idea used by insurance agents to sell large amounts of life insurance. This is the subject of the news article I wrote in May of 2003, which is included in the appendix of this book. When this article was released, it was picked up around the world, including in Germany and Canada. Take a minute to read it in order to gain some insight into some of the discussion here.

When a person retires, they must choose how they will receive their money. The single option is simple. This option gives you the most money monthly, but it has its drawbacks. For example, if you die before your spouse, your spouse gets nothing. You can see this is a difficult choice, since you risk leaving your spouse with no income.

Don't worry, you can also choose the joint option. The joint option gives you about twenty percent less monthly, but if you die before your spouse, he or she will typically get half your monthly income. There are many variations, but these two are the most common.

Let me elaborate with an example. Assume you get $2,000 a month with a single option, and you would get $1,600 a month under the joint option. Okay, that means you pay $400 a month to provide your spouse with $800 a month when you die. However, if your spouse dies before you, your income doesn't increase back up to $2,000 a month. You have to keep paying for a benefit that will never be paid to anyone.

Here is where the benefit of life insurance comes in. I could give you the same $1,600 a month, protect the spouse for the $800, should you die first, and give you back your $2,000 a month if your spouse dies first. This also allows you a legacy to leave to your children, all for about the same cost. Which would you choose? I think it's a no-brainer.

Let's crunch the numbers: $800 a month x 12 months is $9,600 a year. You would need to have enough capital and interest to generate at least the $800 a month. Take $9,600 and divide it by, let's say, 5 percent, and you get a capital need of $192,000 earning five percent to generate the $9,600 per year. The agent recommends that you purchase $192,000 of new life insurance. You gasp! But it sounds good, and it's logical.

This is a great plan, however. If you wait to age 65 to do it, you won't be able to buy the insurance for $400 a month. At this age, the cost would be more like $800 a month. This is where the agent commits malpractice by not explaining the risks and selling you a plan that is not guaranteed. The agent probably didn't give you a permanent guaranteed option choice. Even if the agent had, you would have thought the premium was too expensive.

It is imperative to understand how all the parts of your master plan work together. I have had a number of people realize in my office that their insurance was not guaranteed and was going to terminate soon. I have been able to salvage some of their plans, but most reduce the coverage and take a chance. They have no alternative. They have replaced a guaranteed benefit with a non-guaranteed solution.

If you had purchased an amount of life insurance equal to human life value when you were forty, your problem would already have a solution. You could take the single option, and your spouse would be protected. What rate of return would you put on having this solution? You would have been willing to pay 400 dollars a month in this example. I assure you that buying insurance at forty is easier that at sixty-five. Our strategic master plan will show you how to pay for it with no out-of-pocket cost.

If we look at the whole life illustration on pages 82 and 83, you will see that in about the third year, the cash value increases equal to the premium. Yes, that's right. It's like moving money from money drawer A to money drawer B. In the process, you get the life insurance death benefit. The benefit is not only guaranteed but has the potential to increase. That's good because it helps with inflation and also recovers the first couple years when the cash value is not available to you. Eventually, the cash equals more than you paid and actually has a rate of return between three and 5 percent over your lifetime.

Let's say you purchased the correct amount of insurance, which we now know to be human life value, when you were thirty-five or forty.

Solomon Heubner, who founded the American College in 1928, had a dream to create an institution of higher learning for the insurance industry he also developed the concept of Economic human life value.

It is the economic value of a human being during his or her productive years. Today, we look at multiples of income. Someone making $60,000 a year at age 40 would have a human life value of about $1.2 million.

If you were killed in an accident, your spouse would hire an attorney. His job would be to get your economic human life value awarded to your spouse. Let me ask you a question: Does it matter how you die? Wouldn't you want your family to receive your true-life value, whether you died in an accident or of natural causes?

CHAPTER TEN

REVERSE MORTGAGE

What other benefits can you access through life insurance? One is a reverse mortgage. In a reverse mortgage, the bank loans you money against your house. They give you a lump sum or a monthly income for a negotiated amount and period of time.

These products are promoted for seniors who have little cash and lots of house value. The biggest asset most will have at retirement will be their house. How much will your monthly retirement check be from your biggest asset? A reverse mortgage pays you, and you don't pay anything back unless you leave the house or die. Then the note comes due at the bank. Being forced to sell your house doesn't sound like an attractive plan, does it?

How many people will be able to access this value? Anyone who has life insurance equal to human life value can access it. In this case, the life insurance provides security for you to obtain a reverse mortgage when you need or want to without having to worry that you or your spouse will lose the house when one of you dies.

Let me say this: The reverse mortgage should be considered as a last resort! However, a proper life insurance strategy can make a positive result that can provide tax-favored income.

CHAPTER ELEVEN

TAX SAVINGS

Let's move now to another concept, which I will call, "Pay it out and save the tax." This is a unique concept you will not hear from the financial institutions that promote compounding of money. Accumulation theory and compound interest may not be in your best interest. In fact, they may be hazardous to your financial health.

First, we need to understand how financial institutions make their money. They use our money to make money by being lenders and investors to others. Think of it like this: You get paid on payday, you cash your check, and take the whole amount and put it in a tin can. If you didn't spend any money anywhere, the economy would come to a halt. In a capitalistic society, money has to stay in motion to create more money.

If wealth is created by movements of money, how would you benefit with some amount of interest paid to you for someone else to have the ability to use your money in the multiplier way? You put your money in the bank, and they pay you 5 percent interest. They loan it out four more times and make 20 percent.

Let's say you put $50,000 in a bank account for the next thirty years and earn an average of 6 percent interest. You'll see that the amount of tax you pay on the interest will become greater than what you invested. That's right. You'll pay more in taxes than you put into savings.

Add to the tax the interest you could have earned on the money had you not paid the tax, and the amount is staggering.

Let me start by stressing that compound interest creates increasing tax. Compound tax over your lifetime could possibly cost the average person as much as a million dollars of wealth.

"In previous discussion of how banks make money on our money, we make 5 percent on our money, and they make potentially 20 percent. In 30 years, the 20 percent rate of return on my $50,000 would yield $11,868,816. Think about it; there must be a way for me to make more money on my money."

We live in a society where savings are taxed. Sometimes earnings from savings can be used to pay the life insurance premiums.

Remember, the value each year after the third or fourth year increased the cash value in your policy equal to the annual premium. If that's so, you're basically moving the money from place A to place B and getting the death benefit as a bonus. This cash value grows tax deferred and is available to you by loan for emergencies.

When you borrow from the life insurance company, you are not borrowing your money. Your money is collateral for a loan from the insurance company. The interest savings over your lifetime could be the thousands of dollars the average person pays to banks.

Who do you think is getting richer, You or the banks? If people put all their money into savings and never touch it, is it any wonder why so many people are in debt? The banks want you to depend on them, since this is the primary way they make money.

For example, let's say you have a credit card that has an average balance of 5,000 dollars. If you're paying the credit card company 18 percent interest, wouldn't you rather be paying yourself the 18 percent interest? The interest on $5,000 at 18 percent would be $900. The interest at 7 percent on your insurance policy would be $350. That's a savings of $550, and the net cost here would be about $150. Basically, the $550 could be yours with some discipline and a system to help you manage the process.

The idea of having your money work harder for you increases your rate of return on the money as well as the wealth you will leave behind. This concept by itself has the potential to create hundreds of thousands of dollars just by cost recovery from interest saved. Where does all this money come from, and how can we recover the money we're losing unnecessarily? It's the money that is being earned by the banks and financial institutions that can be recaptured for you. We need a strategic plan that allows us to recapture our hard-earned money from those we borrow from, save, or invest with throughout our lives.

I recommend a book called *The Richest Man in Babylon* by George S. Clason. You must learn how to be a saver, not a borrower.

If you have read this far, you are someone who has the discipline that can be implemented to make this work and help you create a legacy beyond your wildest dreams.

I have talked about individual events motivating everyday situations. When you analyze this, you realize the rate of return is still growing. We're still talking about the same dollars.

Let's review a little. Think of the term insurance premiums and the cost associated with term insurance. If you had participating whole life, the premiums paid for the term insurance would be recovered. If you got the interest each year and used that to pay the life insurance premiums, you would have realized a tax savings. The savings over a lifetime would be in the hundreds of thousands of dollars.

You "finance" everything you buy. You either pay interest to someone else or you give up interest you could have earned.

Creating a strategic plan that gives you control over all your money decisions will recover the lost money on your loans. One such entity can be a life insurance plan. When someone buys a life insurance plan, the contract is very specific to point out who owns the plan (or policy). The insurance company is not the owner! The company is simply the administrator of the plan and must collect premiums and lend money out or make investments to be able to pay the death claims promised. Money is lent to any number of places and types of borrowers, including the owner of the policy, if the owner so desires. The amount of money available to the owner is the entire equity in the policy at the time, less an amount equal to the annual interest that would be due on the loan. In the hierarchy of places where money is lent, the owner ranks first. That gives the policy owner complete control of the funds.

At the end of the year, the life insurance company makes an accounting of the experience that year of the death claims paid, the earnings on premiums collected, and the expenses of running the company. A dividend is declared, which is actually a return to the policy owner of the surplus premium that was collected. Therefore, under tax code, the dividends would not be taxable. When that dividend is credited, it can be used in many ways. The most advantageous choice is you buy additional paid-up insurance at cost, resulting in continuous compounding of an ever-increasing base.

CHAPTER TWELVE

WEALTH ACCUMULATION

Let's move onto your pension plan, be it 401k, 403b, IRA, etc.—all those dollars that haven't been taxed yet. These accounts are the perfect compounding vehicles.

The banks and financial institutions love anyone who puts in money and never withdraws any of it. They get to use your money and never withdraw any of it. They get to use your money all your life and then some. However, when I meet with retirees who have been very good at saving for retirement, they find all their money is locked into the plan and the taxman punishes them when they withdraw it.

You see, they usually have no tax deductions and are in the same tax bracket as when they worked, and some even higher since they were good at saving. Maybe they just have to pay taxes on 8.5 percent of their Social Security income. That's a tax increase if I ever heard one.

Remember the person who sold you on the pension plan. Maybe they were getting you to buy a product and give your money long-term to a well-known financial institution. Ha! Fooled you!

Think about it. What has to happen for you to be in a lower tax bracket? You have to fail financially. If you are successful, you'll probably be in a higher tax bracket. I don't know about you, but my goals center on being in the highest tax bracket. When you go to take out your IRA money, you may get to pay more tax than you deferred on it.

We already know that a retirement plan is the most profitable for banks and financial institutions. Almost all advice is the same: they tell you to max your payments to your IRA, 401K, etc. They tell you your payment is a tax deduction or a tax savings. I hate to be the bearer of bad news, but for most, the tax you don't pay is like a loan—it earns the same interest you do. That means the so-called tax savings may not benefit you at all.

Let me explain further. If you earn $40,000 and put $2,000 into your IRA, your income is reduced to $38,000 and taxed on $38,000. It appears you have saved some taxes. You haven't saved anything, unless it specifically drops you to a lower tax bracket. However, that is unlikely. So you find yourself in a 25 percent marginal tax bracket, and someone said you saved $500. Right? Let me ask you, where is the savings? It's in the plan.

I believe the government loves these accounts. Think about it. You are the best fiduciary the government could have. Their money is co-mingled with yours, growing at the same interest rate. And you wouldn't purposely lose money, would you? To add further injury, you can't get at your money to invest, borrow to pay back to avoid bank interest, or for any other reason without a ten percent penalty until you're fifty-nine and a half. One exception is if you take it out under rule 72T, as an income.

Many are still making decisions about taxes like people did before 1986, when the tax brackets were lowered from a maximum of fifty percent to twenty-eight percent. At the same time, bracket creep, or taking home less money when you get a raise because there were thirteen progressive tax brackets, was eliminated for the most people.

Maximizing your retirement savings in your IRA or other before-tax account will only be good for you if you have an exit strategy. Do you?

CHAPTER THIRTEEN

DISABILITY BENEFITS

What about the disability factor? If you become disabled along the way to retirement and can't work anymore, who is going to put money into your 401K or IRA? Your employer won't keep paying into your plan because you have to have earned income to qualify for a contribution. You may have some disability income coverage, but you still can't afford to put money into your IRA since you're not working. You probably can't afford to save money either, since you probably have experienced a thirty to fifty percent reduction in income and will get no more pay raises.

Let me propose a solution. Instead of putting money into your 401K now, you postpone it for three or four years and pay the premium into a participation whole life policy. This policy includes the waiver of premium benefit, which continues to pay the premium should you become disabled and can't work any longer.

It works as a wealth accumulation continuation. If you become disabled and can't work your regular occupation, after a six months qualification period the insurance company will take over the payment of your premium and continue to pay them until you return to work.

The definition of the disability used by most companies is based on the ability to work your regular occupation for the first two years and then an occupation for five years.

This would guarantee the completion of the amount equal to your pension plan. In addition, you have now placed in motion the assurance that same of the options I've mentioned here will be available to you at retirement.

If you really want to get ahead, you must use all the financial tools and products at your disposal. It's like a symphony orchestra. If you put the leader in the lobby of a hotel and place the different sections of the orchestra throughout the hotel, what would you have?

Using micro-planning is like spreading your financial tools and products around the hotel with no coordination or integration. Needs analysis and micro-planning alone will greatly limit the possible success that is available to all of us. Most of what you hear in the financial world is nothing more than marketing noise.

The federal government abstract statistics state that following people from ages twenty-five to age sixty-five will be as follows: thirty-four have died, fifty-six are dependent on family, friends, churches, charities or the federal government, five are still working because they can't afford to stop, and four are financially secure and one is wealthy.

I ask you, if the information we are getting from the financial education in the marketplace is so good, wouldn't more people be getting ahead? Wouldn't the already successful people be espousing the greatness of the financial world? The fact of the matter is, all I've read of successful people does not collaborate any of the financial education most of us are getting.

Opinion is fact until it is challenged. I'm asking you to challenge the facts and make the people that are giving you advice prove that their advice works. Don't settle for the explanation that it's what everyone else is doing. If everybody is doing it this way, then why aren't more getting ahead?

Be sure your plan can demonstrate that you can use the options I've written about here, including the recovery of opportunity costs, pension maximization, pay it out and save the taxes, reverse mortgage benefits, protecting the 401K and IRA plans, and strategies to pay out your pension plan with minimum taxation.

If your advisor is not showing you how to utilize these concepts, fire him or her and find someone who will. Call me, e-mail firedup@markerman.com, or visit my website, www.1stconsultantsinc.com, and I'll help put you on the road to financial freedom.

EXHIBIT #1

**Why Widows Are Left Destitute, The Loss Of Their Spouses' Life Insurance Benefits, According to 25-Year Insurance Professional.
Thomas W Young, CLU, ChFC**

While the retiree gets more pension money at retirement from choosing the single option versus the joint option, it can leave the spouse without income when he dies, unless the additional money goes to pay for life insurance, says Tom Young, a 25-year insurance professional.

Commonly used, Universal Life Insurance is not guaranteed and may very well expire before the insured dies. Leaving the widow little or no income, says Young. See www.1stconsultantsinc.com.

"A retired couple came to my office recently, and after choosing the single option, six years ago discovered their insurance would terminate within four years," say Young, who is a Certified Senior Advisor specializing in financial consulting with seniors. "We were able to guarantee some of the benefits with some changes," says Young. He warns that many insurance agents are replacing guaranteed benefit with non-guaranteed insurance policies.

Universal Life insurance is being sold under the guise of permanent insurance when it's only a savings account with term insurance deductions. A Penn State University study says only one percent of Term Insurance is ever paid in a death claim, says Young.

Many insurance companies have been sued for "non-disclosure of the non-guarantees" associated with this type of insurance. They continue to sell the same products in the same way, says Young.

What can be done to solve the problem? "There is hope!" These types of policies can be made to work. You have to make adjustment for changes in interest, internal fees, morality charges and they have to be reviewed regularly, says Young.

LIFE INSURANCE: WILL IT PAY WHEN I DIE?

Exhibit # 2

Life Insurance Goal Planning Worksheet
Financial Goals for Life Insurance Policy

Name _____ Date of Birth _____

Rate Class _____

Address _____

Smoker/Tobacco   Y   N   (Circle One)

Check off all that apply:

☐ Projected Cash Value at _____ (ie 65) based on current percentage rate _____.
☐ Projected Cash Value at _____ (ie 65) based on guaranteed percentage rate _____.
☐ Projected Cash Value at _____ (ie 85) based on current percentage rate _____.
☐ Projected Cash Value at _____ (ie 85) based on guaranteed percentage rate _____.

☐ Projected Death Benefit at _____ (ie 65) based on current percentage rate _____.
☐ Projected Death Benefit at _____ (ie 85) based on current percentage rate _____.
☐ Projected Death Benefit at _____ (ie 65) based on guaranteed percentage rat _____.
☐ Projected Death Benefit at _____ (ie 65) based on guaranteed percentage rate _____.

What is the level premium I expect to pay? $ _____

Explain any variations to the level premium (example: pay to 65) or any other variations. Your illustration must match exactly your projected premium. If it does not, explain why.

_____

_____

Exhibit # 2 continued

If more premiums are required to keep policy in force, please explain why.

_____

_____

Important note: any variations to the premium, interest credited, rates, or mortality charges (term insurance cost) will change the projected values. Variable Universal Life, in addition to the above variables, also includes market risk and any possible fees. A 2% annual fee will cost you 43% of your future value in 25 years.

Signature of Policy Owner: _____ Date: _____

Signature of Agent: _____ Date: _____

Exhibit # 3

$ _____ _____ % Current
Your premium   _____ % Guaranteed

Cash Value

                                    Guaranteed   Current
Cash Value at 65 $ _____ $ _____
Cash Value at 85 $ _____ $ _____

Administrative Cost Annual _____
Term Cost at age 60 $ _____ $ _____
Term Cost at age 70 $ _____ $ _____
Term Cost at age 80 $ _____ $ _____

If you would like more information and access to detailed help, please go to our website at www.1stconsultantsinc.com or email your request to info@1stconsultantsinc.com.

APPENDIX A

TERMS AND DEFINITIONS

Accidental Death Benefit: An optional provision that provides an additional payment for loss of life due to an accident that was the direct cause of death. If the additional amount equals the face amount of the policy, this provision is frequently called a "double indemnity" provision. Some companies issue "ADB" in multiples of two or three times the face amount. (See also: double indemnity.)

Accumulated Dividends: Dividends left with the insurer to accumulate at interest. These dividends are generally income tax free, but the interest is taxable as earned.

Actuary: A professional highly educated in a number of fields such as mathematics, statistics, and accounting. An actuary must have superior knowledge as to the underlying principles of life insurance and their mirror image, annuities. Actuaries are responsible for creating new life insurance products and their pricing, value, and profit structures.

Adjustable Death Benefit: Certain life insurance products allow the policy owner to increase or decrease the face amount (within limits and often only with evidence of insurability). For instance, universal and adjustable life policy owners can increase or decrease the amount of death benefit payable by adjusting the level of their premium payments.

Adjustable Life Insurance: Many of the most attractive features of both term and whole life are contained in this highly flexible type of coverage. Premiums, death benefits, duration of coverage, and cash-value levels can all be adjusted (both upward and downward within limits) by the policy owner to meet changing needs and circumstances.

Adjustable Premium: Term applicable to policies where the company has the contractual right to modify or change premium payments under certain specified conditions or to policies where the policy owner has the right to change scheduled premiums in universal or adjustable life.

American College: The only fully-accredited educational institution dedicated exclusively to financial services education. It confers the Chartered Life Underwriter (CLU) and the Master of Science in Financial Services, (MSFS) designations (ChFC), along with Chartered Financial Consultant and (CFP) Certified Financial Planner certifications, among others. It is concerned with continuing-agent training and research in areas related to the life insurance, and other financial services such as estate planning, investments, employee benefits, pensions, retirement planning, and tax planning.

Amount at Risk: The pure insurance element of a life insurance policy. The net amount at risk is equal to the difference between the face value of a policy and its accrued cash value at a given time. The net amount at risk decreases as the cash value increase each year. If the case value becomes the face value, the policy is said to mature or endow.

Annuity: A systematic liquidation of principal and interest over a specified period. An annuity can be measured by a fixed duration (e.g. twenty years) or by the lifetime of one or more persons. A second definition for the term is the contract providing such an arrangement. An annuity can be commercial (e.g., such as the annuity an individual can purchase from an insurer) or private (e.g., a son can promise to pay his father an income for life that the father can never outlive but that ends at the father's death).

Annuity Certain: An annuity that pays a specified amount for a definite and specified period of time, such as five or ten years, with remaining payments going to a designated beneficiary if the annuitant dies before the end of the specified period.

Annuity Certain, Life: An annuity payable for a specified minimum number of periods, or if longer, for as long as the annuitant lives. A combination of an annuity certain and a life annuity.

Assumed Interest Rate: The rate of interest used by an insurance company to calculate its reserves.

Back-End Load: A load is a charge against policy values for business expenses of the insurer in issuing the contract. These charges can be imposed at the inception of the contract (i.e., a "front-end" load) or at the termination of the contractual relationship (i.e., a "back-end" load). In the case of most variable, universal, and current-assumption life insurance products, the load is imposed when the policy is surrendered. Back-end loads typically decrease each year and disappear completely after the number of years specified in the contract.

Beneficiary: The recipient of life insurance proceeds at the death of the insured. A primary beneficiary is first in line to receive that money. A secondary beneficiary is entitled to payment only if no primary beneficiary is alive when the insured dies. Final beneficiaries are those entitled to proceeds if no primary or secondary beneficiaries are alive at the death of the insured. These "backup" beneficiaries are often called "alternate" or "contingent" beneficiaries, since their claims are contingent on the deaths of everyone in the high class of primary beneficiaries.

Capital Stock Insurance Company: An insurance company owned by its stockholders (similar to the ownership of IBM by its shareholders). This form of corporate ownership should be contrasted with a mutual insurance company that is owned by its policy owners and operated solely for their benefit. (See also: mutual company.)

Cash Surrender Value: Cash surrender value is the amount available to the policy owner when a life insurance policy is surrendered. It is also the amount upon which a policy loan is based. In the first eight to ten years after a policy is issued, the cash value is typically the insurer's reserve to meet future liabilities reduced by a surrender charge that enables the insurer to recover expenses incurred in setting up the policy. If a policy is surrendered in later years, the cash surrender value usually equals or closely approximates the reserve value of the policy.

Collateral Assignment: When a life insurance contract is transferred to an individual or other party as security for a debt, this usually temporary assignment does not transfer all policy rights. Under a collateral assignment, the creditor is entitled to be reimbursed only to the extent "his interest may appear," i.e., policy proceeds will be payable only for the amount owned by the policy owner at that time. Any death benefit in excess of the debt owed by the policy owner to the creditor is paid to the policy's beneficiary. (For comparison, see: absolute assignment.)

Conditional Premium Receipt: This is the receipt given to a policy applicant if all or part of the premium is paid at the time of application. This receipt does not provide absolute interim insurance until the company acts on the application if it later approves the application, or more frequently, if the insured meets with the company's rules of insurability for the plan applied for as of the date of the application.

Contestable Clause: Sometimes called the incontestable clause, it is the provision in the insurance contract that states the time (called the contestable period) the insurer has to contest and the grounds under which the policy may be contested or voided by the insurer. By law, the maximum contestable period is two years, but many policies limit the period to one year.

Contingent Beneficiary: One who will receive death proceeds if the principal beneficiary predeceases the insured.

Contract of Insurance: A legally-binding agreement in which an insurer agrees to pay a death benefit upon the death of the insured in return for the consideration of the policy owner's payment of an initial premium and the policy application. Once the insurer issues the contract, the policy owner pays premiums as a condition that precedes the insurer's duty to pay the death benefit upon the demise of the insured. This legally enforceable agreement comprises more than just the policy. The application and any attached supplements, riders, or endorsements form the entire contract.

Conversion: One type of life insurance contract can be exchanged for a different type, assuming the contract is "convertible." For instance, term insurance can be converted to whole life or some other form of permanent insurance. Conversion occurs under a group policy when an insured individual applies for an individual policy without evidence of insurability within a stipulated period of time before the group insurance coverage terminates.

Conversion, Attained Age: The premiums for the converted policy are based on the insured's age attained at time of conversion.

Conversion, Original Age: Premiums for the converted policy are based on the insured's original age at issue. The policy owner must pay the difference in premiums, plus interest, for the time the policy has been in force.

Convertible Term Insurance: A term contract that may be converted to a permanent form of insurance without a medical examination if conversion is made within a limited period, as specified in the contract. The premium is usually based on the attained age of the insured at the time of conversion.

Credit Life Insurance: A policy issued on the life of a borrower with the creditor named as beneficiary to cover the repayment of a loan in the event the borrower dies before the loan has been repaid. Usually written using a monthly decreasing term based on a relatively small, decreasing balance installment loan.

Date of Maturity: The date upon which a life insurance policy endows if the insured is still living.

Death Benefit: The amount stated in the policy as payable upon the death of the insured.

Decreasing Term Insurance: If the face value of term insurance decreases over time in scheduled increments until the policy expires, the insurance is a form of decreasing term. Typically in such policies, the premium remains level.

Deferred Annuity: A series of payments that are not begun until the lapse of a specified period of time or until the annuitant reaches a specific age.

Disability Premium Waiver Insurance: This is an important option or rider in a life insurance policy that provides that if an insured becomes totally disabled for six months or longer, no further premiums will be due, and the policy will be continued in full force until death or recovery occurs. Upon recovery, the policy owner does not have to repay premium payments made by the insurer on behalf of the policy owner during the disability period. WARNING: This is a popular provision, and it can provide tremendous benefit if structured properly. The problem here is there are dozens of different definitions for disability. Example: Gainful employment, any occupation for compensation, your regular occupation, your occupation at time of disability, etc. As you can see, some of the wording in these definitions can make it very difficult to qualify for a benefit, hence you pay a premium for a benefit you most likely couldn't qualify for. The best definition is "your occupation" or "the material and substantial duties of your regular occupation." This definition usually applies for two years, and a few companies have a five-year period, which would be more preferable. After the two or five-year initial period, the best I've seen is an "occupation fitted by education training and experience". Also, be aware that this benefit is totally different in universal life and variable-type products. Get a full explanation before you buy. The term "waiver of premiums" has many different meaning. BEWARE!

Dividend: When a policy participates in the favorable investment, morality, and expense experience of the insurer (so-called "par" policies), the policy owner receives dividends as a refund of an overcharge in premiums. For tax and other purposes, these dividends are considered a return of capital rather than a profit payment. More simply, the insurance company rewards present policyholders for good health and better mortality experience.

Dividend Additions: Participating policies provide that their dividends may be used as single premium to purchase paid-up insurance at the insured's attained age as additions to the amount of insurance specified on the face of the contract. These additions are purchased at net rates, with no commissions or other charges to the policy owner. (See paid-up additions).

Dividend Options: The different ways in which the insured may elect to receive dividends under a participating policy. The dividend options generally include receiving payments in cash, applying them to reduce premiums, purchasing additional paid-up insurance, having them held by the insurer to earn interest for the policy owner, or purchasing additional term insurance.

Evidence of Insurability: A statement or proof of a person's physical condition, occupation, etc. that affect the acceptance of the applicant for insurance.

Expense Charge: In variable, universal life, and other current-assumption policies, all costs are individually deducted and accounted for within the policies. These expense charges are fixed amounts or percentages deducted from gross premiums paid and cash value, as specified in the policy.

Extended Term Option: A nonforfeiture option that provides that the net cash-surrender value of a policy may be used as a net single premium at the attained age of the insured to purchase term insurance at the face amount of the original policy for as long a period as possible.

Family Income Policy: A life insurance policy that combines whole life and decreasing term to provide income protection against the premature death of the family breadwinner. If the insured dies within a specified period, the family will receive a stated amount of income from date of death until the end of the period. The face amount of the policy is then paid to the family.

Family Income Rider: Similar to a family income policy except the decreasing term coverage is written as a rider to a whole life policy rather than as a combination of both coverages.

Family Policy: A policy that combines whole life and convertible term to provide insurance on each family member in units of coverage. Each unit generally consists of $5,000 of whole life on the wage earner, $1,250 of convertible term on the spouse, and $1,000 of convertible term on each child.

Family Rider: An optional policy supplement attached to the insurance policy issued to the head of a family and insuring other members of the family, generally the spouse and children.

FIFO: This term refers to First-In-First-Out and it simply means that first-money-in is your money, and first-money-out is your money, with no tax due. Any gain earned is still in account and won't be taxed until you receive your basis first.

Fifth Dividend Option: Because this option is usually listed after four other possibilities, it is called the fifth-dividend option. If selected, each year the insurer will use the prior year's dividend to purchase (at no commission or expense charge) one-year term insurance up to specified limits (usually no more than the policy's cash value), with the balance applied toward one or more of the other options. The fifth dividend option is useful to maintain level or increasing protection, to keep coverage high even if a policy loan has been taken out, or when the parties are involved in a split-dollar arrangement.

Final Expenses: Costs incurred during a last illness, funeral and burial costs, debts, probate expenses, death taxes, and any other taxes or obligations that must be paid in order to settle the estate of a descendant.

Fixed-Amount Settlement Option: A life insurance policy beneficiary can request that proceeds be paid in regular installments of a fixed dollar amount. The number of payment periods is determined by the policy's face amount, the amount of each payment, and the interest earned. (For contract, see: fixed-period settlement option).

Fixed Annuity: An annuity that provides fixed payments during the annuity period. (For contrast, see: variable annuity).

Fixed-Period Settlement Option: A life insurance settlement option in which the number of payments is set by the payee, with the amount of each payment determined by the amount of proceeds. (For contrast, see: fixed-amount settlement option.)

Flexible Premium Annuity: An annuity, which allows the owner of the contract to vary premium payments (within limits) from year to year.

Free-Look Provision: A provision in life insurance policies that gives the policy owner a stated amount of time (usually ten days) to review a new policy. It can be returned within this time for a hundred percent refund of premiums paid, but cancellation of coverage is effective from date of issue.

Grace Period: Most life insurance contracts provide that premiums may be paid at any time within a period of generally thirty or thirty-one days following the premium due date, during which time the policy remains in full force. If death occurs during the grace period, the insurer will pay the face amount less the amount of the earned but unpaid premium (and any outstanding loan). Generally, an insurer will not charge interest on overdue premiums if they are paid before the end of the grace period.

Graded Premium Life Insurance: To make life insurance premiums more affordable (and therefore marketable), some insurers sell a form of modified life insurance that starts with relatively low premiums, which increase slowly each year. After a period of years, the premium remains level. The death benefit remains level throughout the term of coverage.

Group Life Insurance: A form of life insurance covering a group of persons generally having some common interest or activity, such as employees of the same company or members of the same union or association. Most group insurance is issued using yearly renewable term and do not require medical examinations.

Guaranteed Cash Value: The guaranteed amount available to the insured on surrender of a policy according to a table of guaranteed values scaled to the number of years in which the policy is in force. In a universal or variable policy, there is no guaranteed cash value.

Guaranteed Cost: This is another term for nonparticipating (non par) insurance. Guaranteed cost can also be defined as the maximum costs that can be deducted from cash value under the terms of the policy in universal or variable life contracts.

Guaranteed Insurability Rider: A rider now offered on most life insurance policies that gives the policy owner the right to purchase additional insurance at specified future times without evidence of insurability. Rates are generally based on attained age at the time of purchase.

Guaranteed Interest Rate: The minimum annual rate of interest used in calculating policy reserves from year to year, of annual increases in dividend accumulations, of the interest factor in proceeds held under a settlement option, or the amount payable under the interest income option, etc. This term also refers to the minimum rate credited to cash value in interest-sensitive polices.

Immediate Annuity: An annuity contract that pays the annuity at the end of each period of payment. The interval may be monthly, quarterly, semiannually, or annually.

Increasing Term Insurance: Term life insurance coverage that increases in face value each year (or certain period) from the date of policy issue to the date of expiration. (For contrast, see: decreasing term insurance and level term insurance.)

Individual Life Insurance: Life insurance contract that covers only one insured but that may sometimes cover several people, such as the members of a family, through the use of riders. The term "individual" is often used to distinguish this type of life insurance from group life insurance.

Insurability: The term insurability encompasses all conditions pertaining to an individual that affect his or her health, susceptibility to injury, as well as life expectancy and other factors considered by the insurer in its underwriting and rating process. If the risk is too high, the insurance company will refuse coverage.

Insurable Interest: A person who has a reasonable expectation of benefiting from the continuance of another person's life or of suffering a loss at his or her death is said to have an insurable interest in that life.

Insured: The individual or group covered by the contract of insurance.

Interest-Only Option: A settlement option under which all or part of the proceeds of a policy are left with the insurance company for a definite period at a guaranteed minimum rate of interest. Interest may be paid (usually subject to certain minimums) annually, semiannually, quarterly, monthly, or in some cases, may be added to the proceeds left with the insurer.

Interest-Sensitive Whole Life: A traditional whole life policy with fixed premiums and traditional nonforfeiture values where interest is credited directly to the cash value at current rates. It is often used somewhat erroneously to refer to current-assumption policies. Generally, loads, morality costs, and interest credits are separately stated. The cash value of the policy is the greater of this fund less surrender charges, and the guaranteed cash values.

Joint Life Annuity: A life annuity payable to two or more annuitants that continues payments until one of the two annuitants dies.

Level Premium: A life insurance premium that remains fixed through the life of a policy. It must be large enough so that in early years the insurer will develop a surplus large enough so that in later years—together with interest and future premiums—there will be enough to pay all death claims.

Level Term Insurance: Term life coverage in which the face value remains the same from the date the policy is issued to the date the policy expires. (For contract, see: decreasing term insurance; increasing term insurance.)

Life Annuity: An annuity contract that pays only until the annuitant dies. Payments cease at that time even if the amount paid by the insurer does not equal the total premiums paid by the annuity owner.

Life Expectancy: The average remaining term of life for a number of persons of a given age, according to probability statistics of a morality table.

Life Income Option: One of the settlement options under which the proceeds of a life insurance or annuity policy may be applied to buy an annuity payable to the beneficiary for life.

Life Income with Period Certain Option: A life insurance proceeds settlement option that will pay at least a specified minimum number of periodic installments in a guaranteed amount, whether the named beneficiary lives or dies.

LIFO: Last In First Out, as in, last amount credited is interest so the first out to you is interest and therefore taxable; as opposed to FIFO, which is first in is your premiums and first out is your premiums (basically your money), and therefore there is no tax.

Limited-Payment (limited-pay) Policy: A life insurance policy that provides for payment of the premium for a period of years less than the period of protection provided under the contract.

Minor Beneficiary: A beneficiary who is under the state's legal age of majority, and thus, not considered competent to make certain financial transactions on his or her own. A legal guardian must be appointed to accept death benefits on behalf of a minor beneficiary.

Misstatement of Age: Giving the wrong age for oneself in an application for insurance or for a beneficiary who is to receive benefits on a basis involving a life contingency. Also, a provision in most life policies setting forth the action to be taken if a misstatement of age is discovered after policy issue.

Morality Table: A table of the morality experience of groups of individuals categorized by age and sex that is used to estimate how long a male or female of a given age is expected to live. Some tables are required to be unisex, i.e., those used for actuarial calculations involving qualified pension plans. The morality table is the primary starting point for calculating the risk factor, which in turn determines the gross premium rate.

Mutual Company: A life insurance company that has no capital stock or stockholders. Rather, it is owned by its policy owners and managed by a board of directors chosen by the policy owners. Any earnings in addition to those necessary for the operation of the company and contingency reserves are returned to the policy owners in the form of policy dividends. (For contrast, see: stock company.)

Nonconvertible Term Insurance: A term policy that may not be converted to a permanent policy.

Nonforfeiture Values: Those values or benefits in a life insurance policy that by law the policy owner doe not forfeit, even if he or she chooses to discontinue payment of premiums. It usually includes cash value, loan value, paid-up insurance value, and extended term insurance value.

Nonparticipating Life Insurance: So-called "non-par" life insurance does not pay policy dividends. The policy owner is not in any way an owner and therefore is not entitled to share in any divisible surplus of the company. Any profits from the excess of the premium over the costs of insurance accrue to the non-par company's stockholders, which is fair since they would be the ones to absorb any losses. (For contrast, see: participating insurance.)

Ordinary Life: Also referred to as straight life and whole life insurance. These three synonymous terms refer to the type of life insurance policy that continues during the whole of the insured's life, generally with level premiums payable each year until death or until age on hundred, when the policy endows if the insured is still living.

Paid-Up Additions: A dividend option that allows the policy owner to use policy dividends to purchase paid-up additional insurance on a net single premium basis at the insured's attained age.

Paid-Up Policy: A policy in which the policy owner has completed payments but that has not yet matured. This may be (1) reduced paid-up insurance provided under the nonforfeiture provision, (2) a limited payment policy under which all premiums have been paid, or (3) a policy in which accumulated dividends have been applied to pay the net single premium required to pay up the difference between the policy's reduced paid-up insurance and its face amount.

Participating Insurance: An insurance policy, usually issued by mutual companies that share a portion of the surplus of the company with policy owners through dividends. The dividends represent the difference between the premiums charged and the actual costs (i.e., claims, expenses, earnings, etc.) experienced during the period for which the premiums were charged. (For contrast, see: nonparticipating life insurance.)

Permanent Insurance: Any form of life insurance in which the insured has the guaranteed right to keep the policy in force as long as he or she pays the premium. Also refers to any life insurance policy that builds case value. (For contrast, see: term insurance.)

Preferred Risk: A person whose physical condition, occupation, mode of living, and other characteristics (including the size of policy to be purchased) indicate an above-average life expectancy, and therefore qualifies for a premium rate that is more favorable than that offered to standard risks. (For contrast, see: standard risk.)

Rated: A rated policy is one issued on a substandard risk with higher than standard premiums.

Rating: The premium classification given to a person who applies for life insurance. The term is usually used when an applicant is designated as a substandard risk. A higher premium reflects the increased risk.

Renewable and Convertible Term: Term life insurance offering the policy owner both the option to renew the coverage at the end of the term period and the option (within the term period) to convert it to a permanent form of insurance.

Standard Policy: A policy issued with standard provisions and at standard rates, not rated or with special restrictions.

Standard Risk: A person who meets the insurer's underwriting criteria for standard policies. (For contrast, see: substandard risk; rated.)

Stock Company: A company that is owned and controlled by stockholders rather than policy owners. (See also: mutual company.)

Straight Term: A basic form of term life insurance, written for a specific number of years, having a level premium and automatically terminating at the end of the period.

Substandard Insurance: Life insurance issued at premium rates higher than standard to applicants who are rated or substandard risks. (For contrast, see: standard policy.)

Substandard Risk: A person whose morality risk is greater than average for his or her age. Substandard rating factors include various medical conditions such as diabetes, hypertension, and heart ailments; high risk occupations such as airline pilots, race car drivers, miners, and high-altitude construction workers; high risk avocations or hobbies such as scuba diving or sky diving; detrimental habits or addictions such as smoking, a history of drug use or alcohol abuse; and possible moral turpitude as evidenced by excessive gambling, criminal convictions, and bankruptcy. Substandard risks, if covered at all, are usually charged additional premium.

Suicide Provision: Life insurance policies include a provision that if the insured commits suicide within a specified period, usually one or two years after date of issue, the company is not liable to pay the face amount of coverage. Generally, liability is limited to a return of premiums paid.

Surrender: The policy owner's return of a policy to the insurance company in exchange for the policy's cash surrender value or other equivalent nonforfeiture values. (See also: nonforfeiture values.)

Surrender Charge: In a variable or universal life policy, a special charge is levied on the available cash value to reimburse the insurer for the unrecovered costs of issuing the policy.

Target Premium: The suggested or recommended annual premium for a universal life policy that will maintain the plan of insurance if the actual interest, morality, and expense experience matches the underlying assumptions used to compute the premium.

Terminal Dividend: Dividends that may be payable upon termination of a policy at death, maturity, or surrender for its cash value, usually after the policy has been in force for at least a specified number of years.

Term Insurance: Life insurance protection that expires after a specified term without any residual value if the insured survives the stated period. The protection period may be as short as thirty days (as in temporary insurance agreements) or as long as twenty years or more. (For contrast, see: whole life insurance.) To learn more about Term insurance, visit our website at www.1stconsultantsinc.com

Term Insurance Rider: A form providing term life insurance that is attached to a permanent life insurance policy, with the purpose of increasing the total amount of protection during the term period.

Universal Life: A flexible-premium, current-assumption, adjustable death benefit that accumulates cash value. Unlike traditional products, universal life completely separates the protection element from the accumulation element of the policy. For more detailed information on universal life, visit our website at www.1stconsultantsinc.com.

Vanishing Premium: A feature in some cash value policies whereby the premium, which is based on premium amount and assumed interest rates, will end after a specified period of time, usually as a result of applying dividends as additional premiums.

Variable Annuity: An annuity that invests the contract holder's funds in security-type investments and does not guarantee the level of payments. Instead, payments may fluctuate up and down in relation to the earnings and market value of the assets in a separate account. Thus, the investment risk is assumed by the contract holder.

Variable Life Insurance: Life insurance that usually provides a guaranteed minimum death benefit, but the actual benefit paid may be more dependent on the fluctuating market value of investments in the separate account backing the contract value. This generally fluctuates with the market value of the investment portfolio.

Whole Life Insurance: A form of life insurance offering protection for the whole of life, with proceeds being payable at death. Premiums may be paid under a continuous premium arrangement or on a limited payment basis for virtually any desired period of years (e.g., one, ten, twenty, thirty, or to ages sixty or sixty-five. See also: ordinary life.)

Yearly Renewable Term Insurance: A one-year term insurance contract that may be renewed each year, generally at successively higher premiums corresponding to the insured's attained age with no evidence of insurability. The right of renewal may extend to ten years or more or to an age such as sixty or sixty-five.

APPENDIX B

IMPORTANT PROVISIONS TO KNOW

Accidental Death Benefit (ADB): An optional provision that provides an additional payment for loss of life due to an accident that was the direct cause of death. If the additional amount equals the face amount of the policy, this provision is frequently called a "double indemnity" provision. Some companies issue ADB in multiples of two or three times the face amount. (See also: double indemnity.)

Beneficiary: The recipient of life insurance proceeds at the death of the insured is the policy's beneficiary. A primary beneficiary is first in line to receive the money. A secondary beneficiary is entitled to payment only if no primary beneficiary is alive when the insured dies. Final beneficiaries are those entitled to proceeds if no primary or secondary beneficiaries are alive at the death of the insured. These "backup" beneficiaries are often called "alternate" or "contingent" beneficiaries, since their claims are contingent on the deaths of everyone in the higher class of primary beneficiaries.

Cash Surrender Value: Cash surrender value is the amount available to the policy owner when a life insurance policy is surrendered. It is also the amount upon which a policy loan is based. In the first eight to ten years after a policy is issued, the cash value is typically the insurer's reserve to meet future liabilities, reduced by a surrender charge, that enables the insurer to recover expenses incurred in setting up the policy. If a policy is surrendered in later years, the cash surrender value usually equals or closely approximates the reserve value of the policy.

Collateral Assignment: When a life insurance contract is transferred to an individual or other party as security for a debt. This usually temporary assignment does not transfer all policy rights. Under a collateral assignment, the creditor is entitled to be reimbursed only to the extent "the interest may appear," i.e., policy proceeds will be payable only for the amount owed by the policy owner at that time. Any death benefit in excess of the debt owned by the policy owner to the creditor is paid to the policy's beneficiary. (For comparison, see: absolute assignment.)

Contestable Clause: Sometimes called the incontestable clause. The provision in the insurance contract that states the time (called the contestable period) the insurer has to contest and the grounds under which the policy may be contested or voided by the insurer. By law, the maximum contestable period is two years, but many policies limit the period to one year.

Contract of Insurance: A legally-binding agreement in which an insurer agrees to pay a death benefit upon the death of the insured in return for the consideration of the policy owner's payment of an initial premium and the policy application. Once the insurer issues the contract, the policy owner pays premiums as a condition that precedes the insurer's duty to pay the death benefit upon the demise of the insured. This legally enforceable agreement comprises more than just the policy. The application and any attached supplements, riders, or endorsements form the entire contract.

Disability Premium Waiver Insurance: This is an important option or rider in a life insurance policy that provides that if an insured becomes totally disabled for six months or longer, no further premiums will be due and the policy will be continued in full force until death of recovery occurs. Upon recover, the policy owner does not have to repay premium payments made by the insurer on behalf of the policy owner during the disability period. WARNING: This is a popular provision and it can provide a tremendous benefit if structured properly. The problem here is there are dozens of different definitions for disability. Example definitions: include Gainful employment, any occupation for compensation, your regular occupation, your occupation at time of disability, etc. as you can see, some of the wording in these definitions can make it very difficult to qualify for a benefit. Hence, you pay a premium for a benefit you most likely couldn't qualify for. The best definition is "your occupation" or "the material and substantial duties of your regular occupation". This definition usually applies for two years, and a few companies have a five-year period. The best I've seen is an "occupation fitted by education training and experience." Also, be aware that this benefit is totally different in universal life and variable-type products. Get a full explanation before you buy. The term "waiver of premium" has many different meanings. BEWARE!

Extended Term Option: A nonforfeiture option that provides that the net cash surrender value of a policy may be used as a net single premium at the attained age of the insured to purchase term insurance at the face amount of the original policy for as long a period as possible.

Free-Look Provision: A provision in life insurance policies that gives the policy owner a stated amount of time (usually ten days) to review a new policy. It can be returned within this time for a one hundred percent refund of premiums paid, but cancellation of coverage is effective from date of issue.

Grace Period: Most life insurance contracts provide that premiums may be paid at any time within a period of generally thirty or thirty-one days following the premium due date, during which time the policy remains in full force. If death occurs during the grace period, the insurer will pay the face amount less the amount of the earned but unpaid premium (and any outstanding loan). Generally, an insurer will not charge interest on overdue premiums if they are paid before the end of the grace period.

Nonforfeiture Values: Values or benefits in a life insurance policy that, by law, the policy owner does not forfeit, even if he or she chooses to discontinue payment of premiums. It usually includes cash value, loan value, paid-up insurance value, and extended term insurance value.

Suicide Provision: Life insurance policies include a provision that if the insured commits suicide within a specified period, usually one or two years after date of issue, the company is not liable to pay the face amount of coverage. Generally, liability is limited to a return of premiums paid.

By General Agent Todd Langford
Creator of Truth Concepts™

SELLING system

Show Your Clients the TRUTH about IUL versus Whole Life

One of MTL's featured selling systems, Truth Concepts™, is a system of calculators designed to help educate your clients and increase your production by providing objective analysis. By adding TRUTH, you can shift clients' thinking about the advantages and value of whole life versus many other financial vehicles. To save you time, MTL's Century II software integrates directly into Truth Concepts™ software.

In a recent MTL University webinar, I demonstrated how Truth Concepts™ can objectively show the strength of whole life (WL) versus indexed universal life (IUL). Let's take a look.

First, a few basic points summarizing the differences between IUL and WL illustrated policy values:

ILLUSTRATED POLICY VALUES

The IUL proposal language offers potential clients "upside potential with downside protection." Using a 35-year-old male with a $1 million death benefit and a $9,554 premium, an IUL proposal illustrated an ultimate account value of $69 million, which definitely showed the upside potential. How can WL compete with that? By adding TRUTH to the situation we can show what is really occurring on the IUL illustration and the potential pitfalls within the assumptions. The downside is not so apparent until we add objective analysis (left).

The illustration included the mortality charges and expenses for the plan. In order to arrive at the projected account value of $69 million, the annual earnings rate each year, every year with no down years, for 86 years, would need to be 8.21%. This is not a very likely scenario under current conditions.

IUL
- Guaranteed gross minimum crediting RATE
- Current mortality costs
- Current fees and expenses
- 20/30/40 year AVERAGE
- Guaranteed death benefit typically does not last until expected mortality age

— VS —

WL
- Guaranteed minimum net VALUE
- Maximum mortality costs
- Maximum fees and expenses
- CURRENT dividend
- Guaranteed death benefit will last until death or endowment

SELLING system

You can shift clients' thinking about the advantages and value of whole life versus many other financial vehicles.

By adding more TRUTH, the earnings rate can be adjusted to reflect actual market experience using historical data. For years the market earned below 2% or above 12%. The earnings rate is set to that particular floor or ceiling, because these would be potential minimums or maximums, according to the IUL illustration. This further reduces the account value to two-thirds of the original amount.

The IUL proposal language offers potential clients "upside potential with downside protection."

An additional minor change can have a huge impact–just by reducing the ceiling from 12% to 11%, the account is reduced by $12 million (not pictured).

And finally, by adding still more TRUTH, setting the earnings each year to the IUL guaranteed minimums of floor and cap of 2% and 4% respectively, completely changes the picture. Instead of the $69 million account value originally proposed, the policy collapses before mortality age 121. So by using the objective analysis of Truth Concepts™, we can demonstrate the account value swinging from a potential $69 million to an actual guaranteed value of $0.

By using the objective analysis of Truth Concepts™, we can demonstrate the account value of swinging from a potential $69 million to an actual guaranteed value of $0.

You can see by breaking down the components of the IUL illustration, and adding TRUTH to the equation, that the old adage of "there are no deals in insurance" is proven true yet again.

To obtain a free trial of this calculator as well as others available from Truth Concepts™, go to *www.truthconcepts.com/support.php*. A detailed demonstration of IUL vs WL using the calculator is available as an archived session of MTL University on the Agent Web Site under "Events and Training". For more information on this selling and educational system and how it can help you and your clients, see "Truth Concepts™" under "Marketing Support" on the Agent Web Site.

REFERENCE LIST

Unlimited Wealth: The Theory and Practice of Economic Alchemy. By Paul Zane Pilzer

God Wants You to Be Rich: How and Why Everyone Can Enjoy Material and Spiritual Wealth in Our Abundant World. By: Paul Zane Pilzer

Other People's Money: The Inside Story of the S and L Mess. By: Paul Zane Pilzer and Robert Deitz

Economics of Life Insurance. By: Solomon S. Huebner

Richest Man in Babylon. By: George S. Clason

LEAP – Lifetime Economic Accumulation Process. By: Robert Castiglione

The Family Money Farm-The CFO Project. By: Thomas W Young

According to industry sources, forty-one percent of adults in the United States have no life insurance, and thirty-three percent of U.S. families say they don't have enough life insurance to protect their loved ones if a primary wage earner in the family were to die.

When I meet with clients and we "dream in color" about their hopes and aspirations and what they want to see happen, the discussion will often lead to the need for life insurance. I'm always asked "Tom, what is the best policy I can buy?" My response is always that I believe the "best" life insurance policy to have is the one that's in force on the day you die. The life insurance industry has done an amazing job at creating an array of products: term, universal, variable, indexed universal, and whole life. While every client and situation are different, I am convinced that for long-term financial peace of mind, a participating (dividend-eligible) whole life policy offers a flexible foundation with guarantees and living benefits that offer you certainty in an uncertain world. An industry study reported that buyers prefer whole life insurance because"…it's straight forward and offers premium and cash value guarantees, along with lifetime coverage."

The central advantages of a participating whole life insurance policy revolves around the ironclad contractual guarantees: a guaranteed death benefit, which is typically income tax free to beneficiaries; a guaranteed, level premium that will never increase for the life of the contract as long as you continue to pay premiums; guaranteed cash values that accumulate on a tax-deferred basis and will never decline because of changes in the financial markets; and the guaranteed non-forfeiture provisions that allow you long term exit strategies.

I've mentioned that my preference is for whole life policies that are "participating." What this means is that they are offered by a mutual life insurance company in which the policyowners (that's you!) share in the ownership of the company. In a stock company, the shareholders are the "owners" and typically decisions made by management are based on short-term goals. Mutual companies, however, can make decisions based on more long-term objectives. Dividends, by law, are not guaranteed. However, most mutual companies pass on a portion of their earnings once a year to policyowners by distributing dividends. This is why the financial strength, history, and management of the company you choose is very important. Once declared, the dividends are not guaranteed. Once they've been declared and are in your policy, they are yours. This is where the flexibility and living benefits that dividends offer can really enhance your financial world. Whole life policies offer contractual options for dividends, and these options can be changed through the years as your needs change. They can be sent to you in cash, they can reduce the premium, they can purchase more insurance ("paid up additions"), and they can accumulate interest.

MUTUAL TRUST LIFE INSURANCE COMPANY

"We can never be the oldest company. We do not want to be the largest. We must always be the best."
-Edwin A. Olson

Edwin Olson was one of the founders of Mutual Trust. His quote summarizes perfectly the driving principles of Mutual Trust. From the very beginning of the organization, our goals have been simple and realistic. We can't try to do everything or be everything to our producers and our clients because then we would do none of it well. What we have strived to be is the very best at what we do, and the result has been uncommon focus and success in participating whole life and the value it provides to clients. This is what has driven Mutual Trust for 110 years. This is our story.

Our story begins in July of 1883 in the schoolhouse of the First Lutheran Church in Galesburg, Illinois. A group of people met with the purpose of forming a reliable life insurance organization to protect them and their families. The result was the Scandinavian Mutual Aid Association, forerunner to Scandia Life and Mutual Trust Life. Twenty years later, some of those same men met in Chicago to discuss the idea of organizing and building a life insurance company on sound actuarial principles—one that could not be exploited or manipulated through stock ownership. These men posted the $100,000 of guaranty capital required by the State of Illinois Department of Insurance and obtained a charter for Scandia Life. The men were reimbursed for the capital stock, and the company opened for business on April 14, 1905. The mutual structure of the company that would take the name Mutual Trust in 1919 dates back to its very beginning and continues to this day.

Why is that important? Quite simply, priorities. A stock company exists for one primary purpose—to increase shareholder wealth. Where does that leave the clients? At best, second in line. At Mutual Trust, we are owned by our policyholders, so our first priority is to fulfill our obligations to them and to make decisions that will positively affect their long-term financial security. This philosophy has carried Mutual Trust through World War One, after which the company paid back every dollar of extra war premiums that had been charged for war risks. It carried us through the influenza war epidemic of 1918 and the Great Depression. As an example, during President Roosevelt's "bank holiday" in 1933 when all banks were ordered closed, many life insurance companies declared a moratorium on payments to policyholders and beneficiaries because of the increased demand for funds from policyholders. Mutual Trust did not. That tradition continues through the paying of dividends, which we have done for more than one hundred consecutive years and counting.

Another chapter of our story was written in November 2015, when Mutual Trust Financial Group and Pan-American Life Insurance Group announced their merger. It was the first mutual holding company merger in the life insurance industry in more than ten years, and as the Chairman, President, and CEO of the new organization, Jose Suquet commented at the time: "It could be a business school case study for a successful merger." In completing the merger, Pan-American re-established their presence in the U.S. life insurance market and Mutual Trust became part of a larger organization, with the ratings and capital to fuel our future growth.

—Luke Cosme, VP Mutual Trust Life.

www.ingramcontent.com/pod-product-compliance
Lightning Source LLC
Chambersburg PA
CBHW061510180526
45171CB00001B/112